THEOLOGY OF
ORTHODOX LITURGICAL MUSIC

In Memory of
Fr. Thomas Hopko
(+ 2015),

and

Dedicated to
Alexis Kyriak.

THEOLOGY OF ORTHODOX LITURGICAL MUSIC

BY

DAVID BARRETT

FOREWARD BY
FATHER SERGEI GLAGOLEV

ORTHODOX LITURGICAL PRESS
SOUTHBURY, CONNECTICUT
JULY 2018

Library of Congress Cataloging-in-Publication Data
Barrett, David

1956 –

Theology of Orthodox Liturgical Music

Library of Congress Control Number: 2018949472

THEOLOGY OF ORTHODOX LITURGICAL MUSIC

Copyright © 2018 by
David Barrett

Orthodox Liturgical Press
Southbury, CT 06488

All Rights Reserved.

ISBN 978-0-9915905-7-5

Printed in the United States of America.

CONTENTS

FOREWORD xi
PREFACE xiii

1. LITURGY AND
   ORTHODOX LITURGICAL MUSIC 1
   A. SPIRITUAL PREPARATION 1
   B. LITURGICAL PREPARATION 10

2. LITURGY AND MUSIC 15
   A. THE ESSENCE OF ORTHODOX
      LITURGICAL MUSIC 15
   B. MACRO LITURGICS 19
   C. MICRO LITURGICS 21
   D. THE RESURRECTION:
      THE QUINTESSENTIAL
         MACRO LITURGIC 23
   D. THE ESSENCE OF ORTHODOX
      LITURGICAL MUSIC 26
   E. ESSENTIAL LITURGICAL DUALISM:
      THE EUCHARIST AND THE
         LITURGY OF TIME 30

3. THE TRINITARIAN DIMENSION OF ORTHODOX LITURGICAL MUSIC — 33
   A. THE HOLY TRINITY — 34
   B. THE TRINITARIAN DIMENSION OF ORTHODOX LITURGICAL MUSIC — 37
   C. MUSIC AND TEXT — 38
   D. LITURGICAL MUSIC AND ESCHATOLOGY — 41

4. THE SCRIPTURAL DIMENSION OF ORTHODOX LITURGICAL MUSIC — 45
   A. THE PSALTER — 45
   B. THE SINGING OF HYMNS — 87
   C. THE ESSENCE OF SINGING — 117

5. THE LITURGICAL DIMENSION OF ORTHODOX LITURGICAL MUSIC — 139
   A. SINGING AND JOY — 139
   B. SINGING AND THANKSGIVING — 145
   C. SINGING AND GOD — 149
   D. SINGING AND MAN — 155
   E. "...AND FOR THOSE WHO SING" — 158

BIBLIOGRAPHY — 161

FOREWARD

For many years now, we have had books that deal with iconography. We have long needed a book that addresses the theology of our Orthodox liturgical music. Now, that need has been addressed.

This book speaks to the subject of the theology of Orthodox liturgical music based deeply on the sources of Holy Tradition. It brings that theology alive in our discourse. By presenting his text with many and diverse examples from both Scripture and the patristic sources, David Barrett presents a fantastic articulation of the theology of Orthodox liturgical music.

Fr Sergei Glagolev
East Meadow, NY
July 2018

Fr Sergei Glagolev is a renowned music teacher and composer of Orthodox liturgical music.

PREFACE

I have heard, for many years, those leaders in our Orthodox Church who have taken on the ministry as leaders in the area of Church music, stating that we need to develop and articulate the theology of Orthodox liturgical music. The past three decades, they say, have seen the development of the theology of the icon, and the need for a parallel discussion concerning liturgical music is way overdo. The present work is an attempt to address this need.

I was blessed for many years to have Fr. Thomas Hopko as my spiritual father, my teacher and mentor, and my friend. His recently re-published book, **The Spirit of God** (by Orthodox Liturgical Press) is considered by some people to be his best-written work. In that opus, he presents a clear and concise theology of the Holy Spirit, with numerous quotes and examples from both Scripture and the patristic fathers. Therefore, in discussing the theology of Orthodox liturgical music, I have taken the same approach. I hope the reader will find confirmation for the ideas presented here confirmed in the examples quoted here.

May the Lord God provide all of us with the seriousness, open-mindedness, and prayerfulness that are vital to our liturgical ministries, to His glory and the glory of His holy Kingdom!

1
LITURGY AND ORTHODOX LITURGICAL MUSIC

There are many levels of preparation that a choir director needs to participate in before he or she can effectively function in this ministry. The major part of this book addresses the physiological, executional (singing), theoretical (music theory), directional (using the hands for beat patterns and expression), and preparatory (rehearsal) elements required to master the basic skills of conducting a choir. However, two additional, yet essentially vital, areas for a choir director are the need for spiritual and liturgical preparation.

A. SPIRITUAL PREPARATION

Since liturgical singing is a *ministry*, that is, a participation in the two-natured aspect of the Church that, as the Body of Christ, is both divine and human, all Church singers and, especially, choir directors, must be communing Orthodox Christians who actively, consistently, and seriously participate in the life of the Church, as those who have been baptized to die and rise with Christ through living the sacramental life. This includes continuous participation in the Sacrament of Penance (Holy Confession), a regular, prayerful, and disciplined Communion in the Holy Eucharist, and participation in various other Sacraments, as called to (Holy Unction, Holy Matrimony, Holy Orders, etc.). As Leonid Ouspensky wrote in the book, *The Meaning of Icons*:

> "In order to receive and pass on the testimony [of Holy Tradition], the iconographer must not only believe that it is genuine, but must also share in the life, by which the witness of the revelation lived, must follow the same way, that is, be a member of the body of the Church. Only then can he transmit the testimony received consciously and exactly. Hence the necessity for continual participation in the sacramental life of the Church; hence also the moral demands the Church makes of iconographers. For a true iconographer, creation is the way of asceticism and prayer, that is, essentially, a monastic way. Although the beauty and content of an icon are

perceived by each spectator subjectively, in accordance with his capacities, they are expressed by the iconographer objectively, through consciously surmounting his own 'I' and subjugating it to the revealed truth – the authority of the Tradition."[1]

This essential requirement for a serious participation in the life of the Church and the corresponding spiritual preparation on the part of the iconographer is the very same participation and preparation required of the Church musician, singer and director alike. Both iconography and Church singing are considered liturgical ministries, and, as such, require the same disciplines.

These spiritual disciplines result in clarity of mind, which is essential both in the spiritual life and in the task of fulfilling the various ministries of the Church. The following enumerates this clearly:

"There are two means by which we can acquire such clarity of mind: the first and most necessary is prayer, by which we must implore the Holy Spirit to pour His divine light

---

[1] Ouspensky, Leonid and Lossky, Vladimir, *The Meaning of Icons*, trans. G.E.H. Palmer and E. Kadloubovsky, SVS (St Vladimir's Seminary) Press, Crestwood, NY, 1982, p. 42.

into our hearts. This He will surely do, if we truly seek God alone and sincerely strive to obey His will in everything, willingly submitting in all affairs to the advice of our experienced spiritual fathers and doing nothing without asking them.

The second method of exercising the mind is always to examine things and probe deep for knowledge of them, in order to see clearly which of them are good and which are bad. We should judge them not as the world and the senses do, but as they are judged by right season and the Holy Spirit, or by the word of the divinely-inspired Scriptures, or that of the holy fathers and teachers of the Church. For if this examination and deepening of knowledge is right and proper, it will quite certainly enable us to understand clearly that we must with all our heart regard as valueless, vain and false, all that the blind and depraved world loves and seeks."[2]

---

[2] *Unseen Warfare, the Spiritual Combat and Path to Paradise of Lorenzo Scupoli*, edited by Nicodemus of the Holy Mountain and revised by Theophan the Recluse, translated by E. Kadloubovsky and G.E.H. Palmer, introduction by H.A. Hodges, M.A., D.Phil, Professor of Philosophy, SVS Press, Crestwood, NY, 1978, p. 90.

Silence, solitude, and stillness are necessary elements to "quiet" the self, in order to hear the "still, small voice" of God in the heart (1 Kg 19:12):

> "Our heart is, therefore, the shrine of the intelligence and the chief intellectual organ of the body. When, therefore, we strive to scrutinize and to amend our intelligence through rigorous watchfulness, how could we do this if we did not collect our intellect, outwardly dispersed through the senses, and bring it back within ourselves – back to the heart itself, the shrine of the thoughts? It is for this reason that St Makarios – rightly called blessed – directly after what he says above, ads: 'So it is there that we must look to see whether grace has inscribed the laws of the Spirit.' Where? In the ruling organ, in the throne of grace, where the intellect and all the thoughts of the soul reside, that is to say, in the heart. Do you see, then, how greatly necessary it is for those who have chosen a life of self-attentiveness and stillness to bring their intellect back and to enclose it within their body, and particularly within that

innermost body within the body that we call the heart?"[3]

At the St Sergius Orthodox Institute in Paris in 1997, Dr Dimitri Conomos gave a lecture entitled, "Early Christian and Byzantine Music: History and Performance". In the second section, which he called "Liturgical Music and Orthodox Spirituality", Dr Conomos cited three fundamental concepts in Orthodox spirituality that can be made to apply to our Church music. These are the following (these sections are direct quotes from his lecture):

1. **Asceticism** is the call for self-denial, self-dissatisfaction; and the constant yearning for improvement through hard work and energetic application....The Church singer has a sacred

---

[3] St Gregory Palamas, "In Defense of Those who Devoutly Practice a Life of Stillness", *The Philokalia: The Complete Text, Volume IV*, compiled by St Nikodemos of the Holy Mountain and St Makarios of Corinth, translated from the Greek and edited by G.E.H. Palmer, Philip Sherrard, Kallistos Ware, with the assistance of the Holy Transfiguration Monastery (Brookline), Constantine Cavarnos, Dana Miller, Basil Osborne, and Norman Russell, Faber and Faber, London, England, 1995, p. 334.

profession, and this sanctity requires a determination of character, a strong faith, great modesty, and a high sense of integrity. To be a Church singer in an Orthodox Church is to respond to a calling, to a vocation – it demands purity, sureness of faith, and conviction.

2. **Holiness**. And what is meant by the **holiness** of our vocation?...Holiness means otherness, sacredness, apartness – not the common or the ordinary, but the unique, the particular, the uncontaminated.

3. **Apatheia, or "passionlessness"**....This idea of passionlessness is perhaps most reflected in the best Orthodox iconography – where the saint is painted in colours and shapes that transcend everything that is fleshly, sensual, and cosmetic.

These truths are so ontological that they are beginning to be recognized even in the secular world. James Jordan, in his textbook, ***Evoking Sounds***, says the following:

> "Access can only be gained through quiet and stillness within oneself. Quiet solitude must be a daily occurrence. Stillness is a deliberate

choice. You must consciously choose stillness. Unfortunately, the world will not give it to you. Additionally, you must choose stillness over and over again in very difficult situations when it might be easier not to choose stillness. Initially, the discovery of stillness within oneself brings great joy. Soon, however, it brings difficulties and darkness. You will discover that the newfound stillness unmakes personality so you can become a person. By being still, you are able to make yourself less so others can become more. Also (,) by being still, the process of making yourself less allows the music to speak clearly through the ensemble."[4]

This process of "making ourselves less so others can become more" is reminiscent of the words of St John the Baptist (whom our Lord said was the greatest born of woman), when he said, "He [Christ] must increase, but I must decrease" (Jn

---

[4] Jordan, James, *Evoking Sound: Fundamentals of Choral Conducting*, Second Edition, Foreword by Morten Lauridsen, with chapters by Robert W. Rumbelow and James Whitbourn, GIA Publications, Inc., Chicago, IL, 2009 (hereafter referred to as "*Evoking Sound*"), p. 18.

3:30). Through this process, we surrender our entire selves, our egos, our preconceptions, our prejudices, our tastes, likes, and dislikes, to God, so that everything that we do in this ministry of Orthodox liturgical music is for **His** glory, and **not** for ours. The demons of individualism, selfishness, pride, and jealously must be rooted out, and, as our Lord has said, "This kind never comes out except by prayer and fasting!" (Mt 17:31; Mk 9:29). It is easy to become self-centered to the point of making the music an end in itself. For example, even though the Typikon specifies a certain number of stikhera for the day and the saints on "Lord, I Call Upon You," many parish priests, for the pastoral purpose of keeping the length of Vespers to a comfortable level for his parishioners, will limit the singing of stikhera for the saints to only those who are considered major saints, like, St Sergius of Radonezh. However, there those choir directors who eagerly try to talk their pastors into doing all the stikhera called for in the Typikon, even for minor saints whom nobody in the parish has heard of. Surrendering ourselves to God to serve **Him** in **His** Church ("**Your** will be done, on Earth as it is in Heaven!") ensures that things are done "decently and in order" (1 Cor 14:40) in the balanced perspective of humble service in the ministry of Orthodox liturgical music.

B. LITURGICAL PREPARATION

Another vital but often-overlooked area of preparation for choir directors is that of liturgical preparation. There are many directors who have great difficulty in their ministry because they do not know the order of the services beyond the Saturday evening Great Vespers and the Sunday morning Divine Liturgy. Services such as Vigil, Presanctified Liturgy, Funeral, Wedding, Compline, and the services of Holy Week and Pascha cause some directors great anxiety, confusion, and frustration. There are various service books of the Church that can be referred to in order to clarify the order of each particular service. There are also books that give a general outline of the services with the specifics of how they differ in each of the various practices (Russian, Greek, Antiochian, etc.).[5] Finally, *all* choir directors should sit down and go over the services with their parish priest beforehand.

---

[5] Cf. Barrett, David, *Liturgics for Orthodox Liturgical Singing, Volume 1* (July 2015) and *Volume 2* (January 2016), OLP (Orthodox Liturgical Press), Southbury, CT.

Even more essential for every choir director to realize is that liturgical music is ontologically (that is, by its very being) just that: *liturgical*! As Mark Bailey pointed out:

> By principle, liturgy is not an element of music, however important and even essential musicological study may deem that element to be, but music is an element of liturgy. In other words, worship is the raison d'Ltre of the (C)hurch, and worship therefore serves as the point of departure and the point of arrival that should necessarily frame the entire process of musical examination.[6]

This awareness and perspective is not only a necessary prerequisite for all Church musicians (especially choir directors) but also a ***primary factor*** in their ministry:

---

[6] Bailey, Mark, "Toward a Living Tradition of Liturgical Music in North America", *St Vladimir's Theological Quarterly*, Volume 47, Number 2, 2003, p. 192.

To start, the (C)hurch's liturgy or patterns of worship are the primary subjects for examination. In other words, liturgical musicians should seek broadly and in detail to understand the liturgical structures, systems, and points of emphasis that specifically formulate and guide worship in the missionary (C)hurch, and to respond to this understanding with the appropriate musical expression of those elements. Musicians must also take into account the more general inclinations and manifestations of the gathered faithful in response to their communal unity in such a (C)hurch.[7]

The order of the words in the descriptive title of "liturgical music" is thus important: It is the **liturgical** element or component that comes first and is **primary**, and **then** the musical element or component. That is, the musical element is secondary and **subservient** to the liturgical element, which gives the musical element its **only** reason for being. Otherwise, so-called "liturgical music" just ends up being secular music with a religious subject matter that is "performed" in services, rather than being the component that makes the **worship** in

---

[7] *Ibid*, p. 196.

liturgy come alive.[8] Without this vitally essential realization and perspective on the part of Church musicians, the choir director will come to view the music of liturgy as an end in itself, divorced from its ***sole*** and ***primary function*** of giving shape to, enhancing, and manifesting the functions of the liturgical rites. Then, there will be more attention given to the choice of which musical arrangements of a hymn will be sung, based on musical taste and aesthetics rather than on how the setting appropriately reveals the function of the liturgical action the hymn is paired with. This essential component of liturgical preparation is even more lacking on the part of our liturgical musicians nowadays than the spiritual preparation is. It is ***crucial*** that ***all*** choir directors spend a ***great*** deal of time and study in acquiring an authentically Orthodox liturgical perspective, deeply internalizing the fact of the primacy of the liturgical component over the musical one, and examining and evaluating all musical elements, choices, and decisions in deference to the liturgical elements and their functions within the services themselves.

---

[8] *Ibid*, p. 193.

2
LITURGY AND MUSIC[9]

A. THE ESSENCE OF ORTHODOX LITURGICAL MUSIC

There are some affirmations and that can be stated regarding the essence of Orthodox liturgical music.

First and foremost, the name "liturgical music" manifests the ontological reality of this music: that it is primarily, and exclusively, **liturgical!** Its **raison d'etre** is precisely to be an artistically expressive component of the worship in the liturgical services of the Church. Granted, a choir or choral group **may** sing hymnological selections at concerts outside the services themselves; these "concerts" may even take place in the parish church building itself. Yet, at **that** point, the music ceases to be **liturgical** and becomes just another concert "piece" that may be sung alongside Handel's "Messiah." It is **only** in the

---

[9] Portions of this chapter are from chapter 2 of my *Liturgical Theology of Orthodox Liturgical Music*, OLP (Orthodox Liturgical Press), Southbury, CT, January 2017, pp. 15-32.

context of the liturgical services that this hymnology fulfills its true function.

Second, since the liturgical services are in total harmony with the Scriptures, the dogmas, and the Holy Tradition of the Church, Orthodox liturgical music not only becomes a mode of expression of the theology of the Church, but its very manner of celebration must be in total harmony with that theology. We have already spoken above about how Pascha, the Feast of feasts celebrating the Resurrection of Christ, is the theological nexus of the liturgical year, and that, therefore, the singing of our liturgical music should be done in a paschal manner. Other aspects of the very being of the Church should also be manifested in the celebration of our liturgical music. For example, keeping in mind our Lord's command to "make disciples of all nations, baptizing them in the Name of the Father, and of the Son, and of the Holy Spirit" (Mt 28:19), another ontological aspect of the Church is her **missionary** calling. **Therefore**, the manner in which the liturgical music is celebrated will be specific to the time and place in which the Church (especially as found in the local parish) finds herself. The "style" and manner of Church singing in a 21st-century parish in America should certainly be different from an 18-century parish in Russia or a 16th-century parish in Antioch!

This also influences how our hymnology is composed and arranged. The specific melodic arrangements, whether they be from a "traditional" chant system (such as Byzantine or Kievan) or a free-composed melody, as well as the essential nuances of text settings, are all vital elements in the missionary component of Church singing. For instance, artificially "stuffing" an English text into a musical setting that was arranged for Greek or Slavonic, will make the setting unintelligible and unprayerful. Taking the time and effort to set English texts to the music in such a way as to correctly accentuate the text and enhance its inherent meaning will reap rich liturgical rewards in the clarity, intelligibility, prayerfulness, and liturgical function of the hymnology.

As mentioned in the previous chapter, an essential component of our liturgical worship is its **eschatological dimension**. Again, all aspects of our liturgical music, from its composition, arrangement, and style of celebration, should manifest this eschatological ontology of liturgy and lift the members of the worshipping community to the reality of the Kingdom of God.

Third, Orthodox liturgical music should be formatted and celebrated according to its **liturgical function!** For instance, all litanies have a dialogical aspect to them, where the priest or deacon chants the petition, and the worshipping community responds with its word of affirmation, be it "Lord, have mercy," "To You, O Lord," or "Amen." Distinct from this, the times of liturgical worship that center around movement and action, such as processions, entrances, and the receiving of Holy Communion, have traditionally been accompanied by responsorial Psalmody, especially in the early Church. The specific function of the liturgical component being celebrated at any given moment of the services therefore determines the type, format, and function of the liturgical hymnology accompanying that component. This crucial and symbiotic relationship between function of liturgical component and format of liturgical music was, alas, lost in the consciousness of the Church for a long time, and has recently (thank God!) been rediscovered by Church liturgists and musicians.

B. MACRO LITURGICS

There are two vitally important ways to look at, study, and evaluate the specifics of our liturgical services: macro liturgics and micro liturgics.

Macro liturgics is the method of studying elements or groups of elements from the liturgical **ordo** of services. As the name implies, this encompasses large portions of the services.

For example, one group of liturgical elements that goes together to make a unified "set" is the group that involves the Scriptural elements at the Divine Liturgy. This begins with the Prokeimenon, which introduces the Epistle reading, then the Epistle reading itself, followed by the "Alleluia!" Verses, which introduce the Gospel reading,[10] the Gospel reading itself, and, finally, the Sermon. These five elements comprise one liturgical "unit," so to speak. In the ancient Church, both the Prokeimenon and the "Alleluia!" Verses, like other elements of the Divine Liturgy, were celebrated in what is called the **"responsorial Psalmody"** format, that is, the people

---

[10] Hopko, Thomas, Podcast series *Worship in Spirit and Truth*, Ancient Faith Radio, podcast for 18 September 2013, "Allelujah, Allelujah, Allelujah."

would sing a refrain from the Psalm and then a reader would chant the verses of the Psalm *in their entirety*, one at a time, between the singing of the refrain.[11] So, for example, the Resurrectional Prokeimenon in tone 1 comes from Psalm 32,[12] which has twenty-two verses. The people would begin by singing the refrain, then they would sing it twenty-two more times, once after each chanting of a Psalm verse by the reader.

The same is true for the "Alleluia!" Verses. Staying with a Sunday where tone 1 is celebrated, the reader would, in the ancient Church, chant a *triple* "Alleluia!", and the people would respond by singing a *triple* "Alleluia!". The reader would then chant the verses of the Psalm *in their entirety*, one at a time, between the singing of the *triple* "Alleluia!". Here, for the Sunday of tone 1, the reader would chant, one-by-one, all fifty verses of Psalm 17. This longer rendering of the Prokeimenon and the "Alleluia!" Verses in the "responsorial

---

[11] Taft, SJ, Robert F., *Beyond East and West: Problems in Liturgical Understanding*, Second Revised and Enlarged Edition, Pontifical Oriental Institute, Rome, Italy, 2011 (hereafter referred to as *"Beyond East and West"*), p. 197.

[12] The Psalms are here numbered according to the Septuagint.

Psalmody" format was done in order to prepare the people spiritually for hearing the Scriptural readings in the Epistle and the Gospel, respectively. It is done that way today in many monasteries, and some parishes are beginning to implement this early Church restoration.

C. MICRO LITURGICS

Micro liturgics is the study of elements or groups of elements in the liturgical services occurring simultaneously. As the name suggests, this involves liturgical elements occupying a small amount of time in the services.

One example of this is the Entrance Hymn for the Vesperal Liturgy of Holy Saturday. Some arrangements of this hymn are in a melismatic setting, that is, having multiple notes per word or syllable. Other settings that have misaccentuation of the text could have this problem resolved by adding more notes (longer melismas) to the setting. Some people question doing this because of the procession that will occur during the Entrance. However, what these people forget is that the Eucharistic Entrance for this particular Vesperal

Liturgy, just like the entrance for the Presanctified Liturgy, has **no** commemorations made. The entire Entrance is done by the clergy and the servers in **<u>total</u> silence**. Therefore, if a few extra notes for an extended melisma **is** called for, there is not the usual concern that there will be not enough time for the clergy to do the commemorations before the Entrance procession concludes because, once again, there are **no** commemorations chanted.[13] This is a good illustration of how the elements of micro liturgics interact with one another and can lead to intelligent decisions regarding the celebration of the services.

    Some people misuse these two terms. They use the term "macro liturgics" to refer to elements that are appropriate for liturgical services and "micro liturgics" to refer to elements that are not appropriate for liturgical services. It seems more appropo to refer to the former elements (those that **are** appropriate for liturgical services) as "liturgical" and the latter elements (those that are **not** appropriate for liturgical services) as "para-

---

[13] Cf., Barrett, David, *Composing and Arranging Orthodox Liturgical Music*, OLP, July 2017, for a further-detailed explanation of this example.

liturgical," and leave the terms "macro liturgics" and "micro liturgics" to be used as presented here.

D. THE RESURRECTION: THE QUINTESSENTIAL MACRO LITURGIC

The concept of macro liturgics goes beyond just large portions of the liturgical services. In fact, in its ultimate size, it encompasses the entire liturgical year itself.

Pascha, the Resurrection of our Lord, God, and Savior, Jesus Christ, is the quintessential macro liturgic! It is the Feast of feasts, around which everything in the liturgical year and all the services revolve. While the Sundays of the liturgical year are numbered as a certain Sunday after Pentecost (due to bringing the fulness of the Kingdom, which Pentecost celebrates, to the "regular time" of this fallen world), the Resurrection remains **the** focal center of the liturgical year (the Oktoechos cycle of the eight tones begins anew each year on Pascha, starting with tone 1):

"Although the first of September is considered the start of the Church year, according to the Orthodox Church calendar, the real liturgical center of the annual cycle of Orthodox worship is the feast of the Resurrection of Christ. All elements of Orthodox liturgical piety point to and flow from Easter, the celebration of the new Christian Passover. Even the 'fixed feasts' of the Church (,) such as Christmas and Epiphany (,) which are celebrated according to a fixed date on the calendar (,) take their liturgical form and inspiration from the Paschal feast."[14]

"This is the starting point of our understanding of the sanctification of time. It is the Orthodox experience, which goes back to the (A)postles themselves, that in the center of our liturgical life, in the very center of that time which we measure as **year**, we find the **Feast of Christ's Resurrection**. What is Resurrection? Resurrection is the appearance in this world, completely dominated by time and(,) therefore(,) by death, of life that shall have no end. The One (W)ho (R)ose again from the dead does not die anymore. In this world of ours, not somewhere else, not in any 'other' world, there

---

[14] *Worship*, p. 70.

appeared one morning (S)omeone (W)ho is beyond death and yet *in* our time. This meaning of Christ's Resurrection, this great joy, is the central theme of Christianity; and it has been preserved in its fullness in the liturgy of the Orthodox Church. There is much truth expressed by those who say that the central theme of Orthodoxy, the center of all its experience, the frame of reference for everything else in her, is the **Resurrection of Christ**....Though it may seem strange to you, it is important to realize that every Sunday is a little Easter. I say 'Little Easter,' but it is really 'Great Easter.' Every week the Church comes to the same central experience: 'Having beheld the Resurrection of Christ...' Every Saturday night, when the priest carries the Gospel from the altar to the center of the church, after he has read the Gospel of the Resurrection, the same fundamental fact of our Christian (F)aith is proclaimed: CHRIST IS RISEN!...This is the heart of our (F)aith; and it is only the reference to Pascha, as the end of all merely natural time and the beginning of the *new* time, that we can understand the whole liturgical year."[15]

"The Church is the entrance into the (R)isen life of Christ; it is communion in life eternal, 'joy and peace in the Holy Spirit.' And it is the expectation of

---

[15] *Liturgy and Life*, pp. 76-77 (emphasis in the original).

the 'day without evening' of the Kingdom; not of any 'other world,' but of the fulfillment of all things and all life in Christ….But(,) I know that in Christ this great Passage, the **Pascha** of the world has begun, that the light of the 'world to come' comes to us in the joy and peace of the Holy Spirit, for **Christ is (R)isen and life reigneth**."[16]

"It is the worship of the Church that was (,) from the very beginning and still is (,) our entrance our entrance into, our communion with, the **new life of the Kingdom**. It is through her liturgical life that the Church reveals to us something that which 'the ear has not heard, the eye has not seen, and what has not yet entered the heart of man, but which God has prepared for those who love Him.' And (,) in the center of that liturgical life, as its heart and climax, as the sun whose rays penetrate everywhere, stands **Pascha**. It is the door opened every year into the splendor of God's Kingdom, the foretaste of the eternal joy that awaits us, the glory of the victory which already, although invisibly, fills the whole creation: 'death is no more!' The entire worship of

---

[16] Schmemann, Alexander, *For the Life of the World: Sacraments and Orthodoxy*, SVS Press, Crestwood, NY, 2002 (hereafter referred to as "*For the Life of the World*"), p. 106 (emphasis in the original).

the Church is organized around Easter, and (,) therefore (,) the liturgical year, i.e., the sequence of seasons and feasts, becomes a journey, a pilgrimage towards Pascha, the ***End***, which is at the same time the ***Beginning:*** the end of all that which is 'old'; the beginning of the new life, a constant 'passage' from 'this world' into the Kingdom already revealed in Christ."[17]

So, we can see, from these excellent examples, that Pascha, the Resurrection of Christ, is at the heart of our liturgical year. Yet, it is even deeper than this. Christ's Resurrection, His ***Pascha***, permeates the very services themselves, even those that we deem, in our hearts and our minds, to be "negative," "sad," or dealing with things of the "fallen" world. The following two examples illustrate this point clearly.

First of all, both the Funeral service and the Memorial, after the initial doxology ("Blessed is our God...!") and the singing of the Trisagion, go immediately into the singing of "Alleluia!", with interspersed verses chanted by the priest. And the singing of "Alleluia!" is ***always*** a liturgical expression

---

[17] Schmemann, Alexander, *Great Lent: Journey to Pascha*, SVS Press, Crestwood, NY, 1974 (hereafter referred to as "*Great Lent*"), p. 13 (emphasis in the original).

of ***joy!***[18] Furthermore, towards the end of both the Funeral and the Memorial, there is a prayer the priest chants that begins, "O God of spirits and of all flesh...!" And the exclamation of this prayer begins, "For, **You** (meaning, Christ) **are the <u>Resurrection</u>**, the Life, and the Repose of Your servant, _____, O Christ our God...!".

    The second example is from the Vespers of Holy Friday. Everyone will agree that this is **the** most solemn day of the entire liturgical year, the day of Christ's Crucifixion on the Cross! Nothing can be considered more "negative," "sad," or "fallen" than this world's rejection of our Lord and His murder by the most shameful death imaginable on the Cross. ***Yet***, in the midst of all this "negativity," "sadness," and "fallenness," the light of **the Resurrection** still shines ***liturgically***! This is celebrated at the singing of the stikhera on the Apostikha, where the verses interspersed by the reader are **the same exact <u>resurrectional</u> verses chanted by the reader at every Saturday evening <u>Resurrectional</u> Vespers throughout the liturgical year:** "The Lord is King! He is robed in majesty!"; "For, He has established the world, so that it will never be moved!"; and, "Holiness befits Your house, O Lord. Forevermore!".

---

[18] Ibid, p. 138, note 5.

Therefore, even here, in the midst of the pathos of Christ's Crucifixion, His Resurrection begins to shine forth for us!

Now, what does all this mean for choir directors and Church singers? Well, if the light of Christ's Resurrection shines through every liturgical nook and cranny of all the services of the liturgical year, then, to properly follow the liturgical theology of the Orthodox Church, **_all_ the singing at _all_ of the services of the entire liturgical year should be sung resurrectionally!** This does **not** mean that we should sing "Open the Doors of Repentance" and the Kanon of St Andrew of Crete in a boistrous manner. But, it **does** mean that we should sing these and all other hymnology not in a defeatist, morbid manner, but keeping the joy, the hope, and the faith of Christ's Resurrection in mind! One way to do this is to pitch the music in a higher key, to get a "brighter" sound. Another way is, without rushing the pace of the singing, to move it along so that the "rhythm" of the service doesn't drag, in order for the service itself to be imbued with some life and energy. This is the first and most essential element of our liturgical theology as it applies to the celebration of our services in the singing of our Orthodox liturgical music!

E. ESSENTIAL LITURGICAL DUALISM: THE EUCHARIST AND THE LITURGY OF TIME

There is an essential liturgical dualism that exists in the Church. What is key to remember is that **this liturgical dualism has lived in the Church from the very beginning!**[19] This dualism consists of the presence of the Eucharist, which is the manifestation of the Kingdom of God here on Earth and, therefore, of the Eschaton, that which will be consummated at the Parousia for all eternity, and, at the same time, the presence of the Liturgy of Time, of those services that sanctify the time of our life in this world, here and now. As Fr Schmemann points out in the pages of his book referenced in the footnote below, many liturgiologists mistakenly thought that the Liturgy of Time was incompatible with the *eschatology* of the Church, that eschatology was a renunciation of the world that had chosen autonomy from God, sin, and death over

---

[19] Schmemann, Alexander, *Introduction to Liturgical Theology*, SVS Press, Crestwood, NY, 1986, pp. 4-89, especially pp. 64-80.

communion with God, and that, therefore, the Liturgy of Time could only have developed in the flowering of monasticism in the 4th century. Fr Schmemann corrects this skewed perspective by showing that, just as the New Testament is the fulfillment of the Old Testament, the Christian concept of eschatology fulfills the Jewish concept of eschatology. Both the Jews and the Christians awaited the coming of the Messiah. The "newness" of Christianity was that this awaiting was now fulfilled in the coming of Christ. Yet, the Kingdom ***still*** awaits ***complete*** fulfillment in the Second Coming of Christ. Therefore, since the current time of the Church is dualistic in the sense that the Kingdom is "already" here but "not yet" fulfilled, so this dualism is expressed ***liturgically*** with ***both*** the Sacrament of the Kingdom, the Eucharist, ***and*** the Liturgy of Time simultaneously taking place in the life of the Church. This dualism, since it is liturgical, therefore goes to the heart of the essence of the liturgical services: those of the Liturgy of Time (Vespers, Matins, etc.) function for us as we Christians being ***in statio***, that is, in that state of watchfulness that Christ commanded us to be in, since we would not know when the Master would be coming ***again the <u>second</u> time!*** In fact, our daily lives contain an experience, on a daily basis, of the

Death and Resurrection of Christ: we experience a death each night when we enter that state of unconsciousness called "sleep," and we experience a resurrection each morning when we wake up, fully alive for a new day. Perhaps that is why, with the Resurrection of Christ being **_the_** central event in the life of the Church, that, of all the daily services, Matins is the most key and the most central! This hypothesis is strengthened by a passage from St Cyprian of Carthage: "We should pray in the early morning, that, by means of our morning prayer, the Resurrection of the Lord might be recalled."[20] The Eucharist, then, is our experience of the fulness of the Kingdom, given to us now in anticipation, but with its **_full_ consummation** taking place at the Parousia! These two complementary functions of the liturgical dualism of eschatology, the "already" and the "not yet," **_must_** be kept in mind and manifested **_liturgically_** in the various services of the Orthodox Church!

---

[20] St Cyprian of Carthage, *De Oratione*, p. 35, quoted in Schmemann, op. cit., p. 82.

3
THE TRINITARIAN DIMENSION OF ORTHODOX LITURGICAL MUSIC[21]

Theology is defined as words adequate to God. It is the experience of our Faith, lived out in liturgy and in our daily lives. Theology, then, is not an academic enterprise promulgated by stuffy intellectuals in university libraries. It is the articulation of that which makes up our very being and of everything in creation. It is "the expression of our *experience* of being baptized into the life of the Father and the Son and the Holy Spirit".[22] To use St Paul's term, it is our life "*in Christ*".

A theology of our liturgical music, then, is the expression and explanation of it as it really is, as it really functions, and as it is really experienced in its proper perspective.

---

[21] This chapter is a reprint of chapter 9 in my *Elementary Music Theory for Orthodox Liturgical Singing*, OLP, Southbury, CT, January 2015, pp. 212-224.

[22] Archimandrite Vasileios, *Hymn of Entry*, SVS (St Vladimir's Seminary) Press, Crestwood, NY, 1984, p. 19.

A. THE HOLY TRINITY

Everything in creation is an expression, a revelation, of God. To understand something in creation, liturgical music, for example, we must first understand God as He really is. This is revealed in the dogma of the Holy Trinity. The word **dogma** means official teaching,[23] and is something that is revealed by God to the Church, usually over a long period of time. The dogma of the Holy Trinity took four hundred years to formulate.

According to Orthodox doctrine, the one God of the Christian Faith is the Person of God the Father.[24] It is **not** the Trinity. This is not to say that the Son and the Holy Spirit are not divine. They are equally divine with the same divinity as that of the Father, and are as eternal and perfect as the Father is. They share the same **nature** as the Father, but They are different **Persons**. They are **what** the Father is, but not **Who** He

---

[23] Hopko, Thomas, *The Orthodox Faith: Volume I: Doctrine and Scripture (An Elementary Handbook on the Orthodox Church)*, SVS Press, Yonkers, NY, 2016 (hereafter referred to as "*Doctrine*"), pp. 45-49.

[24] Ibid.

is. "Hear, O Israel, the Lord, He is God, the Lord, He is **One**" (Dt 6:4).

Being the one God, the Father is the **Source** of all that there is, *including* the Son and the Holy Spirit. This is why They are referred to as "the Son *of* God" and "the Spirit *of* God". Being the Source and Father is the main characteristic of God the Father. He is the **Content** of everything.

The Son of God, the Word (**Logos** in Greek), is the very **Expression** of the Father's Own Being. He is the Image of the invisible God (Col 1:15), the very Icon of His being. The Son Himself reveals that to us: "He who has seen Me has seen the Father" (Jn 14:9). The Son expresses the very Content of God.

The Holy Spirit, the Spirit of God, is the Communicator of the Life of the Father, the **Giver** of this Life.[25] He is the Activator, the **Vivifier**, Who communicates, activates, and electrifies the Life of God, making it be **alive**. The Holy Spirit vivifies the Life, the Content of God the Father.

The Holy Spirit, along with vivifying the Life of God, has other Personal characteristics. He is, in one

---

[25] Stikheron to the Holy Spirit, "O Heavenly King". See also Hopko, Thomas, *The Spirit of God*, OLP, Southbury, CT, 2018.

sense, the "hidden Person" of the Holy Trinity: "He remains **unrevealed, hidden**, so to speak, by the gift in order that this gift which He imparts may be fully ours, adapted to our persons".[26] The Son is revealed to us directly as the Man, Jesus Christ. The Father is revealed to us in the Person of the Son, Who is the perfect Image of the Father. The Person of the Holy Spirit is revealed to us more subtlely, in the multiplicity of persons who make up the Church: "...for the multitude of saints will be His image".[27]

Another Personal characteristic of the Holy Spirit, however, is that of **inspiration**. Even though He remains humbly "hidden", it is through His inspiration that the prophets spoke the Word of God revealed to them, that the human authors of the Books of the Bible communicated the Word of God to us **in words**. It is through His inspiration that Christ was baptized, that He was led into the wilderness to be tempted, that He cast out devils, healed the sick, fed the multitude in the wilderness, raised the dead, and was led to the Cross.

---

[26] Lossky, Vladimir, *The Mystical Theology of the Eastern Church*, SVS Press, Crestwood, NY, 1976, pp. 166-167.

[27] Ibid, p. 173.

B. THE TRINITARIAN DIMENSION OF ORTHODOX LITURGICAL MUSIC

If everything in creation is an expression of God, then each thing has a trinitarian dimension to it. This is true, also, of liturgical music. There are, therefore, three aspects of liturgical music. The first of these is the *content* of the hymn, the reality that is being expressed in word and song. This is analogous to the Person of God the Father, Who is the Content of everything. This is also true because the content of every hymn, whether it be a doxology praising God or a troparion of the life of one of His saints, is **God Himself**.

The second characteristic of liturgical music is the *word*. Without words, the music carries no meaning in and of itself (this is why instruments are canonically forbidden in the Orthodox Church; every sound must have a meaning, and meaning can only verbally be communicated in words). This is analogous to the Person of the Son, Who is the Word of God, Who reveals God to us. As the Word of God leads us to the Content of divinity, to the Person of God the Father ("No one comes to the Father but by Me" [Jn 14:6]), so the words of the hymn lead us to its content, to communion with God.

The third characteristic of liturgical music is the *music* itself. This is analogous to the Person of the Holy Spirit, Who vivifies and gives Life to all, even God. The music gives life and vivifies the words of the hymn, leading us through them to the content, to God. We approach and commune with God the Father through the Son in the Holy Spirit. We approach and commune with the content of our hymnography through the words in the music.

C. MUSIC AND TEXT

This analogy can be contemplated more deeply. If the words of our hymnography are analogous to the Personal characteristics of the Son and the music is analogous to the Personal characteristics of the Holy Spirit, what do the Son's and the Holy Spirit's characteristics say about the characteristics of the words and the music.

The Son of God is undoubtedly the Person of the Holy Trinity Who reveals Himself the most directly. It is the Son Who was incarnate of the Virgin; it is the Son Who was baptized, walked among men, taught, healed, exorcized, raised the dead, was crucified, buried, resurrected, ascended into Heaven, and sent the Comforter into the world. Since He is the image of the invisible God (Col 1:15), then God Himself (the Father) is invisible, as is the Holy Spirit. "No man has seen God at any time; the only Son, Who is in the loins of the Father, He has made Him known" (Jn 1:18).

If, then, the Son is the One Who is in the forefront, Who stands out and is primary (no one comes to the Father but by Him, and it is He (the Son) Who sends the Spirit), **then it is the words, the text, of our hymnography that must be in the forefront, that must stand out and be primary!**

Likewise, the Holy Spirit is the Person of the Trinity Who is "hidden", Who is in the background. Yet, while not calling attention to Himself, He nevertheless is the One Who vivifies, makes alive, and inspires. Therefore, the musical element of our hymnography must *not* call attention to itself, must not overpower and cloud the text and the meaning of the text. It is not the music that leads us to the content of the hymnography (the Gospels states that "No one comes to the Father but by Me [the Son]"; it does not say that "No one comes to the Father but by the Spirit"), but rather, the music makes the text come alive and, through that vivification, inspires us to enter into the text, embracing, contemplating, and praying with the text, to make our hearts one with its content.

The difficult task of the choir director (after mastering the musically technical skills outlined in this book), the ***cross*** that needs to be taken up at each service and rehearsal, is to walk the narrow road of allowing the music to vivify the text, to inspire us to enter into its reality, without overpowering, clouding, or dominating the forefront of our hymnography. This is realized in many ways. First of all, it is realized in the choice of arrangements to be sung. Many arrangements are ***not*** liturgical for the very reason that the music is so ornate that the text and its content, the prayer, the doxology, the enumeration of the Faith, is lost or buried. Other arrangements may be musically appropriate, but the way the music is set to the text takes away from its contemplation by misaccenting the words. Putting half notes on unaccented syllables makes the singing cumbersome, unprayerful, and non-liturgical.

Once appropriate, liturgical arrangements have been chosen, the choir director must be watchful that the execution of the singing is not done in a manner that is sentimental, what modern jargon would call "schmaltzy". Using extreme emotionalism in the style of singing distracts and detracts from the concentration of the words and their content. There is a unity, a harmony among the three Persons of the Holy Trinity. There also needs to be a unity, a balance, a harmony between the three aspects (content, text, and music) of our Orthodox hymnography.

D. LITURGICAL MUSIC AND ESCHATOLOGY

Finally, our Orthodox liturgical music is just that, it is *liturgical*. *Liturgy* means "common work" or "common action",[28] and our hymnography is an essential part of that work. It is only when the people of God gather together, assemble **as Church** do they **constitute** the Church, becoming the very Body of Christ which is the Church. And it is only in these divine gatherings, within this divine Assembly that our hymnography manifests and becomes what it is in its very nature, *liturgical* music.

---

[28] Hopko, Thomas, *The Orthodox Faith: Volume II: Worship (An Elementary Handbook on the Orthodox Church)*, SVS Press, Yonkers, NY, 2016, p. 146.

What, then, is goal, the main thrust, of liturgy and, therefore, of liturgical music? What takes place at the Divine Liturgy? What is the apex of this service that is called "the Eucharist"? Is it not the Eucharist itself, the partaking of the Body and Blood of Christ, what has been called the Sacrament of sacraments? And, if this is so, why has this sacrament been given to us? Why did Christ "institute" the Holy Supper before His life-saving Passion? The answer is given to us by the Lord Himself during that very Meal: "And I assign to You, as My Father assigned to Me, a **Kingdom**, that you may eat and drink at **My** Table in **My** Kingdom" (Lk 22:29-30). It is this Kingdom that is the Goal, the End, and the Fulfillment of all things. It is this **Eschaton** (the Last Things) that is the focus and whose content is the Kingdom of God, the Life lived **in Christ**, in perfect communion with God the Father and the Holy Spirit. Thus, this Kingdom, which is given to us in the Church, the Church Herself, Her life, Her liturgy, and Her music, are all **eschatological**. It is this Life in communion with God in His Kingdom that is the **content** of our Orthodox hymnography.

"And, when they had sung a hymn, they went to the Mount of Olives" (Mt 26:30; Mk 14:26). From the beginning, music has been inexorably linked with the Eucharist and with the Kingdom. **Eucharist** means "thanksgiving", and **thanksgiving** is at the very heart of this Life of the Kingdom. In thanksgiving, Christ fed the multitudes in the wilderness, offered up prayer to His Father, and accepted voluntarily His life-saving Passion. It is in and through this *ministry* of liturgical music that we enter into this thanksgiving of Christ, making it our own and the very content of our life: "...but be filled with the Spirit, addressing one another in psalms and hymns and spiritual songs, singing and making melody to the Lord with all your heart, always and for everything giving thanks in the Name of our Lord Jesus Christ to God the Father" (Eph 5:19-20).[29]

---

[29] Epistle reading for the second Day of the Holy Trinity, the Day of the Holy Spirit.

4
THE SCRIPTURAL DIMENSION OF ORTHODOX LITURGICAL MUSIC

A. THE PSALTER

The Psalter has been called "the hymnal of ancient Israel."[30] The Psalms are linked with liturgical singing. There are 150 Psalms in the Psalter, and more than a third of them, 54 Psalms in all, are dedicated "[t]o the Choirmaster."[31]

The Psalms, Prayer, and Meditation

The Psalms are also linked to the spiritual life. They are directly related to prayer and meditation.

---

[30] *The New Oxford Annotated Bible with the Apocrypha*, Expanded Edition, Revised Standard Version, Oxford University Press, New York, NY, 1982, p. 656.

[31] These Psalms (numbered according to the Septuagint) are Psalms 4-6, 8-13, 17-21, 30, 35, 37-41, 43-46, 48, 50-61, 63-69, 74-76, 79-80, 83-84, 87, 108, and 138-139.

"Pray with meditation and calm, and chant Psalms with understanding and proper measure, and you will be raised on high like a young eagle."[32]

"It was said of the same Abba John that, while returning from the harvest or from meeting with the elders, he devoted himself to prayer, meditation and psalmody until he had restored his mind to its original order."[33]

"'The high mountains are for the stags' (Psalm 102:18). And again, 'The voice of the Lord prepares the stags' (Psalm 27:9). If, then, by the teaching of the Lord and the sacred canons of asceticism you become as a stag, and stripped bare of

---

[32] Eusebius of Caesarea, *De oratione* 82, in McKinnon, James, *Music in Early Christian Literature* (hereafter referred to as "*Music*"), Cambridge University Press, New York, NY, 1987, p. 59.

[33] Isidore of Pelusium, *Apophthegmata Patrum*, Ioannes Curtus 35, in *Music*, p. 62.

the graves of evil, having become emboldened against the figurative serpents, you kill them. Do not remain at this level, but strive to ascend to the high mountains through continuous psalmody, through the practice of perfection, and through that blessed contemplation that which nothing is higher. Thus, 'Blest are the pure in heart, for they will see God' (Mt 5:18), and 'The Lord has set me upon high places' (Psalm 16: 34)."[34]

The Psalter and the Daily Cycle

Being "the hymnal of ancient Israel," the Psalter with its Psalms is the oldest form of prayer we have in the Church. And, being a **hymnal**, it is also the oldest **songbook** we have in the Church. The Christian Church, being the "new Israel," developed her liturgical services and forms of

---

[34] Nilus of Ancyra, Epistle, III, 38, to Callinicus, monk, in *Music*, p. 91.

worship from the old Israel. This especially included the widespread use of the Psalter in all of the services. One could say, with reverence and respect, that the liturgical services of the early Church were **saturated** with the singing of the Psalms. Even now, there are fixed Psalms for the various services:

- Psalm 103[35] is the main Psalm that is chanted at Vespers.
- The 6 Psalms at Matins are Psalms 3, 37, 62, 87, 102, and 142.

The fixed Hours of the liturgical day also have fixed Psalms appointed to them:

- The 1st Hour has Psalms 5, 89, and 100.
- The 3rd Hour includes Psalms 16, 24, and 50.
- The 6th Hour consists of Psalms 53, 54, and 90.
- The 9th Hour has Psalms 83, 84, and 85.

---

[35] Again, throughout this book, the numbering of the Psalms is according to the Orthodox tradition of the Septuagint.

Other services in the Daily Cycle also have certain Psalms associated with them:

- The service of Little Compline consists of Psalms 50, 69, and 142.
- Finally, Nocturns includes Psalms 50, 120, and 133.

The Psalter and the Divine Liturgy

The Sunday Divine Liturgy has fixed Psalms associated with it, as well:

- The 1st Antiphon contains Psalm 102.
- The 2nd Antiphon is from Psalm 145.

Verses from Psalm 50 are interspersed during the Anaphora at the time of the Prayer of the 3rd Hour

("Create in me a clean heart, O God, and put a new and right Spirit within me!" and "Cast me not away from Your presence, and take not Your Holy Spirit from me!").

The Prokeimenon and the "Alleluia" verses for the Sunday Divine Liturgy are also taken from the Psalter. There is a different set for each of the 8 tones:

Tone 1

- Prokeimenon – Psalm 32.
- "Alleluia" Verses – Psalm 17.

Tone 2

- Prokeimenon – Psalm 117.
- "Alleluia" Verses – Psalm 19.

Tone 3

- Prokeimenon – Psalm 46.
- "Alleluia" Verses – Psalm 30.

Tone 4

- Prokeimenon – Psalm 103.
- "Alleluia" Verses – Psalm 44.

Tone 5

- Prokeimenon – Psalm 11.
- "Alleluia" Verses – Psalm 88.

Tone 6

- Prokeimenon – Psalm 27.

- "Alleluia" Verses – Psalm 90.

Tone 7

- Prokeimenon – Psalm 28.
- "Alleluia" Verses – Psalm 91.

Tone 8

- Prokeimenon – Psalm 75.
- "Alleluia" Verses – Psalm 94.

When the Divine Liturgy is celebrated on a weekday, what are known as the "ordinary antiphons" are sung:

- The 1st Antiphon consists of Psalm 91.
- The 2nd Antiphon is from Psalm 92.
- The 3rd Antiphon contains Psalm 94.

The Psalter and the Feasts of the Lord

Then, on the major feasts of our Lord, special antiphons are sung for these feasts:

Exaltation of the Holy Cross (14 September):

- The 1st Antiphon contains Psalm 21.
- The 2nd Antiphon is from Psalm 73.
- The 3rd Antiphon consists of Psalm 98.
- The Prokeimenon is from Psalm 98.
- The "Alleluia verses are from Psalm 73.
- The Communion Hymn is from Psalm 4.

Christmas (25 December):

- The 1st Antiphon is from Psalm 110.
- The 2nd Antiphon consists of Psalm 111.

- The 3rd Antiphon contains Psalm 109.
- The Prokeimenon is from Psalm 65.
- The "Alleluia verses are from Psalm 18.
- The Communion Hymn is from Psalm 110.

Theophany (6 January)

- The 1st Antiphon contains Psalm 113.
- The 2nd Antiphon is from Psalm 115.
- The 3rd Antiphon consists of Psalm 117.
- The Prokeimenon is from Psalm 117.
- The "Alleluia verses are from Psalm 28.
- The Communion Hymn is from Titus 1:11.

Meeting of the Lord (2 February)

- The 1st Antiphon consists of Psalm 44.
- The 2nd Antiphon is from Psalm 44.
- The 3rd Antiphon contains Psalm 44.
- The Prokeimenon is from the Magnificat (Luke 2).
- The "Alleluia verses are from the Song of St Symeon (Luke 2).
- The Communion Hymn is from Psalm 115.

Palm Sunday

- The 1st Antiphon contains Psalm 115.
- The 2nd Antiphon is from Psalm 115.
- The 3rd Antiphon is from Psalm 118.
- The Prokeimenon is from Psalm 116.
- The "Alleluia verses are from Psalm 97.

- The Communion Hymn is from Psalm 117.

Pascha

- The 1ˢᵗ Antiphon consists of Psalm 65.
- The 2ⁿᵈ Antiphon is from Psalm 66.
- The 3ʳᵈ Antiphon contains Psalm 67.
- The Prokeimenon is from Psalm 117.
- The "Alleluia verses are from Psalms 101 and 32.
- The Communion Hymn is the regular Sunday one, "Receive the Body of Christ! Taste the Fountain of Immortality!"

Ascension

- The 1ˢᵗ Antiphon consists of Psalm 46.

- The 2ⁿᵈ Antiphon is from Psalm 47.
- The 3ʳᵈ Antiphon contains Psalm 48.
- The Prokeimenon is from Psalm 56.
- The "Alleluia verses are from Psalm 46.
- The Communion Hymn is from Psalm 46.

Pentecost

- The 1ˢᵗ Antiphon contains Psalm 18.
- The 2ⁿᵈ Antiphon is from Psalm 19.
- The 3ʳᵈ Antiphon consists of Psalm 20.
- The Prokeimenon is from Psalm 18.
- The "Alleluia verses are from Psalm 32.
- The Communion Hymn is from Psalm 142.

Transfiguration

- The 1ˢᵗ Antiphon consists of Psalm 65.
- The 2ⁿᵈ Antiphon is from Psalm 47.
- The 3ʳᵈ Antiphon contains Psalm 124.
- The Prokeimenon is from Psalm 103.
- The "Alleluia" verses are from Psalm 88.
- The Communion Hymn is from Psalm 88.

The Psalter and the Feasts of the Theotokos

The four feasts of the Theotokos that are part of the Twelve Major Feasts also have Psalmody as part of their festive celebration:

The Nativity of the Theotokos (8 September)

- The Prokeimenon is from the Magnificat (Luke 2).
- The "Alleluia" Verses are from Psalm 44.
- The Communion Hymn is from Psalm 115.

The Entrance of the Theotokos into the Temple (21 November)

- The Prokeimenon is from the Magnificat (Luke 2).
- The "Alleluia" Verses are from Psalm 44.
- The Communion Hymn is from Psalm 115.

The Annunciation (25 March)

- The Prokeimenon is from Psalm 95.
- The "Alleluia" Verses are from Psalm 71.
- The Communion Hymn is from Psalm 131.

The Dormition of the Theotokos (15 August)

- The Prokeimenon is from the Magnificat (Luke 2).
- The "Alleluia" Verses are from Psalm 131.
- The Communion Hymn is from Psalm 115.

The Psalter and the Lenten Cycle

The Psalter also figures in extensively with the services of the Lenten cycle. For the sake of brevity, we will only present here those Psalms for the Sunday Liturgy:

Sunday of the Last Judgment (Meatfare)

- The Prokeimenon is from Psalm 146.
- The "Alleluia" Verses are from Psalm 94.

Sunday of the Expulsion of Adam from Paradise (Cheesefare)

- The Prokeimenon is from Psalm 75.
- The "Alleluia" Verses are from Psalm 91.

1st Sunday of Great Lent

- The Prokeimenon is from the Song of the Three Holy Youths.
- The "Alleluia" Verses are from Psalm 94.
- The Communion Hymn is from Psalm 32.

2nd Sunday of Great Lent

- The Prokeimena are from Psalms 11 and 48.
- The "Alleluia" Verses are from Psalms 90 and 36.
- The Communion Hymn is from Psalm 111.

3rd Sunday of Great Lent

- The Prokeimenon is from Psalm 27.
- The "Alleluia" Verses are from Psalm 73.
- The Communion Hymn is from Psalm 4.

4th Sunday of Great Lent

- The Prokeimena are from the Oktoechos

and Psalm 149.
- The "Alleluia" Verses are from the Oktoechos and Psalm 91.
- The Communion Hymn is from Psalm 111.

5*th* Sunday of Great Lent

- The Prokeimena are from the Oktoechos and Psalm 95
- The "Alleluia" Verses are from the Oktoechos and Psalm 71.
- The Communion Hymn is from Psalm 131.

The Psalter and God

The Psalter also links God directly with music, as is evident from Psalm 117:14: "**The Lord is** my

Strength and **_my Song!_** He has become my Salvation!" Here, God not only is the content of music, **He Himself is Music!** The Church fathers link the Psalter directly to Christ:

> "The Psalms also come to our aid on this point, not the psalms of that apostate, heretic, and Platonist, Valentinus, but those of the most holy and illustrious prophet, David. **He sings among us of Christ**, and, through him, **Christ indeed sang of Himself**."[36]

> "There should be no doubt that **the things mentioned in the Psalms must be understood** in accordance with the teaching of the Gospel, such that, regardless of the person in whom the prophetic spirit has spoken, it should nonetheless be referred to in its entirety to recognition **of the coming of our Lord, Jesus Christ**, His Incarnation, Passion, and Kingdom, and to the glory and excellence of our own resurrection...For,

---

[36] Tertullian, *De carne Christi* xx, 3, in *Music*, p. 45 (emphasis added).

prophecy as a whole is woven together with allegories and types, through which are revealed all the mysteries of the only-begotten Son of God as He is Born in the flesh, suffers, dies, arises again and, along with those glorified by Him for their belief in Him, reigns in eternity and judges all others. And, because the scribes and Pharisees did not acknowledge that the Son of God was Born in the flesh, and so denied everyone access to the prophetic understanding, they are condemned thus by the Lord: 'Woe to you who are learned in the Law, for you have taken away the key of knowledge: You have not entered in, and those entering in, you have hindered.' (Luke 11:52.)"[37]

---

[37] Hilary of Poitiers, *Instructio psalmorum* 5, in *Music*, p. 122 (emphasis added).

Psalmody and the Spiritual Life

The Church fathers also talked about the connection between psalmody and the spiritual life of Christians. Clement of Alexandria spoke of the link between psalmody and blessing:

> "Just as it is appropriate for us to praise the Creator of all before partaking of food, so too is it proper while drinking to Him as the beneficiaries of His creation. **For a Psalm is a harmonious and reasonable blessing**, and the Apostle calls a Psalm a spiritual song."[38]

Psalmody also can be beneficial when dealing with one's passions, as well:

---

[38] Clement of Alexandria, *Pedagogus II,* iv, in *Music,* p. 34 (emphasis added).

"Reading, keeping vigil and prayer focus the wandering mind. Hunger, toil and solitude quell inflamed desire. **Psalmody, patience and pity arrest seething anger.** And these are to be practiced at the appropriate time and in good measure, for what is excessive and ill-timed is not lasting, and what does not last is harmful rather than beneficial."[39] **"Psalmody lays the passions to rest and causes the stirrings of the body to be stilled**; prayer prepares the mind to perform its proper activity."[40]

St Basil the Great and Psalmody

St Basil the Great articulates what the Psalms do for us:

---

[39] Evagrius Ponticus, *Praktikos* xv, in *Music*, p. 58 (emphasis added).

[40] Evagrius Ponticus, *De Oratione* 83, in *Music*, p. 59 (emphasis added).

> "A Psalm is tranquility of soul and the arbitration of peace; it settles one's tumultuous and seething thoughts. It mollifies the soul's wrath and chastens its recalcitrance. A Psalm creates friendships, unites the separated and reconciles those at enmity. Who can still consider one to be a foe with whom ones utters the same prayer to God! Thus psalmody provides the greatest of all goods, charity, by devising in its common song a certain bond of unity, and by joining together the people into the concord of a single chorus."[41]

He clearly elucidates the essence of the Psalms:

> "All Scripture is inspired by God for our benefit; it was composed by the Spirit

---

[41] Basil the Great, *Homilia in psalmum* I, 2, in *Music*, pp. 65-66.

for this reason, that all we men, as if at a common surgery for souls, might each of us select a remedy for his particular malady. 'Care', it is said, 'makes the greatest sin to cease'. Now, the prophets teach certain things, the historians and the Law teach others, and Proverbs provides still a different sort of advice, but the Book of Psalms encompasses the benefit of them all. It foretells what is to come and memorializes history; it legislates for life, gives advice on practical matters, and serves in general as a repository of good teachings, carefully searching out what is suitable for each individual."[42]

St Basil also says that, because God is the Source of the Psalms, by singing them we raise ourselves to Him:

---

[42] Basil the Great, *Homilia in psalmum* I, in *Music*, p. 65.

"While there are many musical instruments, the prophet adapted this Book to that called the Psaltery, which, as it seems to me, displays resonating within itself the grace of the Spirit from on high, because it alone among musical instruments has the source of its sound in its upper parts. While the brass of the cithara and lyre responds to the plectrum from below, **this Psaltery has the Source of its harmonious strains from above**, so that we too might be anxious to pursue higher things, and not brought down to the passions of the flesh by the pleasure of song."[43]

He elaborates further on the transforming aspect of the Psalms:

---

[43] Basil the Great, *Homilia in psalmum,* 1, 2, in *Music,* p. 66.

> ***"So the Psalm was written** for the Jews of that time, **but for us who are to be transformed**, who exchange polytheism for piety and the error of idolatry for the recognition of Him Who made us, who choose moderation under the Law in place of illegitimate pleasure, and who substitute Psalms, fasting, and prayer, for auloi, dancing and drunkenness."[44]

He also speaks of the Psalms nourishing our souls as food and drink nourish out bodies:

> "Long since have you arrived at this sacred shrine of the martyrs, and from the middle of the night you have propitiated their God with hymns, persevering to the middle of this day, awaiting my arrival. Now is the reward at hand for you who have preferred the vexation of the martyrs and the worship

---

[44] Basil the Great, *Homilia in psalmum*, lix, 2, in *Music*, pp. 66-67 (emphasis added).

of God to sleep and relaxation....So as
not to distress you by detaining you
any longer, *I will first discourse briefly
upon the Psalm you were singing as I
came upon you, nourishing your souls*
with words of consolation as in me lies,
and then dismiss you all for the care of
your bodies. Now what was it that you
sang? 'I have loved,' he says, 'because
the Lord will hear the voice of my prayer'
(Psalm 115: 1)[45]

He speaks of the Psalms used at the various Hours as renewing our souls throughout the day:

"Daybreak is a set time for prayer so
that we dedicate the first stirrings of
soul and mind to God, and take up no
other consideration until made joyous
by the thought of God; as it is written:
'I remembered God and was delighted'

---

[45] Basil the Great, *Homilia in psalmum*, cxiv, 1, in *Music*, p. 67 (emphasis added).

(Psalm 76: 4); and so that the body will busy itself with no work before accomplishing that which was written: 'For, to You will I pray, O Lord, in the morning You will hear my voice. In the morning I will stand before You, and will see.' (Psalm 5: 3) Again, at the 3rd Hour, the brethren must come together and assist at prayer, even if they each happen to be occupied in different tasks. They must remember the gift of the Spirit, granted to the Apostles at the 3rd hour, and worship all together in one accord.... We judge prayer to be necessary at the 6th Hour in imitation of those holy ones who said: 'Evening and morning and at noon, I will speak and declare; and He will hear my voice.'
(Psalm 54: 17) And so that we might be safe from misfortune and the midday demon, the 90th Psalm is recited at this time. That we must pray at the 9th Hour is related to us by the Apostles themselves in their Acts, where it says that Peter and John went up to the temple 'at the hour of prayer,

the 9th.' (Acts 3: 1) At the day's end, thanksgiving should be offered for those things given us in its course as well as those things done rightly, and confession should be made of any lapses, deliberate or inadvertent.... And again as night begins, we must ask that our rest will be free from sin and evil fantasy; again, the 90th Psalm must be recited at this hour. For the middle of the night, Paul and Silas have told us that prayer is necessary, as the account in their Acts narrates: 'But about midnight, Paul and Silas were singing hymns to God;' (Acts 16: 25) and as the Psalmist says: 'In the middle of the night I arose to praise You for the judgments of Your righteousness.' (Psalm 118: 62) And, finally, it is necessary to anticipate the dawn and rise for prayer so that one is not caught by the day asleep in bed, according to the saying: 'My eyes have awoken before daybreak, that I might meditate on Your words.' (Psalm 118: 148) Not one of these times is to be overlooked by those who have earnestly dedicated their lives to the glory of God and Christ Himself. Moreover, I think it useful to have diversity and variety in the prayer and psalmody at these appointed times, because somehow the soul is frequently bored and distracted by routine, **while by change and variety of the psalmody and prayer at each hour its desire is renewed and its concentration restored.**"[46]

St John Chrysostom and Psalmody

Other Church fathers have also commented on the various aspects of psalmody. One of them is St John Chrysostom:

"When the day is about to begin, they [the monks] finally leave off from their activity, and as we begin our tasks, they have a period of rest....Again, after they

---

[46] Basil the Great, *Regulae fusius tractatae*, *Interragio* xxxvii, 3-5, in *Music*, pp. 67-68 (emphasis added).

have completed their morning prayers and hymns, they turn to the reading of the Scriptures (while some have also been educated in the copying of books). Each occupies a single allotted cell, he practices silence throughout, no one speaks frivolously, no one says anything at all. Then they observe the third, the sixth, the ninth hours, and the evening prayers, dividing the day into four parts, **with each part filled, as they honor God with psalmody and hymns**. So, while all others are lunching, laughing, playing, and bursting from gluttony, they are patiently occupied with their hymns. Then, after sitting for a short while, or rather concluding everything with hymns, each goes to bed upon a straw pallet made up for rest only, not luxury."[47]

The saintly father associates the singing of psalmody with the action of the Holy Spirit:

---

[47] John Chrysostom, *In I Timotheum*, Homily xiv, 4, in *Music*, p. 88 (emphasis added).

"Since this sort of pleasure is natural to our soul, and lest the demons introduce licentious songs and upset everything, God erected the barrier of the Psalms, so that they would be a matter of both pleasure and profit. For, from strange songs, harm and destruction enter in along with many a dread thing, since shat is wanton and contrary to the Law in these songs settles in the various parts of the soul, rendering it weak and soft. **But, from the spiritual Psalms can come considerable pleasure**, much that is useful, much that is holy, and the foundations of all philosophy, as these texts cleanse the souls **and the Holy Spirit flies swiftly to the soul who sings such songs**."[48]

He also stresses the importance of singing the Psalms as a defense against the devil:

---

[48] John Chrysostom, *In psalmum* xli, 1, in *Music*, p. 80 (emphasis added).

> "I say these things, not so that you alone sing praise, but so that you teach your children and your wives also to sing such song, not only while weaving or while engaged in other tasks, but especially at table. **For, since the devil generally lies in wait at banquets**, having as his allies drunkenness and gluttony, along with inordinate laughter and an unbridled spirit, **it is necessary especially then, both before and after the meal, to construct a defense against him from the Psalms**, and to arise from the banquet together with wife and children to sing sacred hymns to God."[49]

The saint even associates the singing of psalmody with the sanctification of the tongue:

---

[49] John Chrysostom, *In psalmum* xli, 2, in *Music*, p. 80 (emphasis added).

"And even if you do not understand the meaning of the words, for the time being teach your mouth to say them, ***for the tongue is sanctified by the words alone whenever it says them with good will***. Once we have become confirmed in this custom, we will not neglect this congenial duty either deliberately or through indifference, as custom will compel us to fulfill this grateful service every day, even if unwillingly. Nor will any complaint concerning this singing arise, even if one has grown old, is still a child, has a rough voice, or is altogether ignorant of rhythm. This is because what is sought here is a sober soul, an alert mind, a contrite heart, sound reason and a clear conscience. If having these, you enter into the holy choir of God, you will be able to stand beside David yourself."[50]

---

[50] John Chrysostom, *In psalmum* xli, 2, in *Music*, p. 81 (emphasis added).

Other Church Fathers and Psalmody

There are more references to psalmody from various other Church fathers. St Gregory of Nazianzus speaks of how singing psalmody now in this world leads to singing psalmody in the Kingdom:

> "The place before the great sanctuary, where you will stand after Baptism, is a sign of future glory; **the psalmody with which you will be received is a foreshadowing of future psalmody.**"[51]

St Gregory of Nyssa has also commented on the importance of psalmody:

---

[51] Gregory of Nazianzus, *Oration XL, In sanctum baptisma* 46, in *Music*, p. 72 (emphasis added).

"And by no means was she [Macrina] ignorant of the Book of Psalms, completing each portion of psalmody at the appropriate times; and, upon rising from her bed, when taking up her chores and leaving off from them, when beginning to eat and leaving the table, when going to bed and arising for prayers – **everywhere she had with her the Psalter, like a good companion which one forsakes not for a moment.**"[52]

An unknown saint recommends singing psalmody throughout the night in order to maintain the watchfulness of the soul:

"In the middle of the night arise and hymn the Lord your God, for at that hour our Lord Arose from the dead and hymned the Father, for which

---

[52] Gregory of Nyssa, *Life of Macrina* 3, in *Music*, p. 73 (emphasis added).

reason He has enjoined us to hymn God at that hour. After rising say first this verse: 'I rose at midnight to give praise to You, for, the judgments of Your righteousness,' (Psalm 118: 62) and pray, and begin to say the entire 50th Psalm until you finish; and these things have been prescribed for you to carry out each day. Say as many Psalms as you can while standing, and after a Psalm pray and make a prostration, with tears acknowledging your sins to the Lord and asking that He forgive you. And with each three Psalms say the "Alleluia." And if there are virgins with you, let them also sing the Psalms and perform the prayers one by one. At dawn say this Psalm: 'O God my God, to You do I watch at break of day; for You my soul has thirsted;' (Psalm 62: 2) and at daybreak: 'All you works of the Lord, bless the Lord, sing hymns;' (Daniel 3: 57) 'Glory to God in the highest;' (Luke 2: 14) and what follows."[53]

This point is made by two other saints. One of them is Callinicus:

"And during Lent he [Hypatius] ate every second day, confining himself, and chanting the Psalms and praying at daybreak, the third hour, the sixth, the ninth, the lighting of lamps, late evening, and the middle of the night, according to the saying: 'Seven times a day I have praised You for the judgments of Your righteousness.' (Psalm 118: 164) 3 Chanting Psalms, then, seven times in the course of the day and night, he completed one hundred Psalms and one hundred prayers."[54]

---

[53] Anonymous, *De virginitate xx*, in *Music*, p. 74.

[54] Callinicus, *Life of Hypatius xxvi, 2-3*, in *Music*, p. 92.

The other saint to make this point is Eusebius of Caesarea:

> "'Make Your mercy heard to me in the morning.' (Psalm 148: 2) Amid temptations we need God's mercy, and in our prayers we vigilantly devote ourselves to its arrival, especially at the early morning hour, so that it can be said: 'God, my God, to You do I watch at the break of day.'" (Psalm 62: 2)[55]

Just like St John Chrysostom, St Nilus of Ancyra saw the advantage of psalmody in warding off the wiles of the devil:

---

[55] Eusebius of Caesarea, *In psalmum cxlii, 8*, in *Music*, p. 98.

"The demon of fornication, in the manner of a licking puppy, is wont to cling to the one he tempts, so as not to be cast out. But, it is possible for you – it is a matter of your prerogative and intention – either to nourish him with the work of dishonor or **vigorously to put him to flight with prayer and psalmody**, with fasting and vigils, and will sleeping on the ground."[56]

Finally, St Niceta of Remesiana looks upon the singing of psalmody as a spiritual sacrifice:

"Rightly does the same prophet [David] urge everybody and everything to the praise of God Who rules over all: 'Let every spirit praise the Lord.' (Psalm 150: 5) And promising that he himself would

---

[56] Nilus of Ancyra, *Epistle*, II, 159, in *Music*, p. 91 (emphasis added).

be the one who praises, he said: 'I will praise the Name of God in song, I will magnify Him in praise; and it will please God better than a young calf that brings forth horns and hoofs.' (Psalm 68: 31-32) Behold what is superior, behold the spiritual sacrifice, greater than all the sacrifices of victims. And justly so; if there indeed the irrational blood of animals was poured out, here is offered the reasonable praise of the soul itself and a good conscience. Rightly did the Lord say: 'The sacrifice of praise will glorify Me, and there is the way by which I will show him the salvation of God.' (Psalm 49: 23) Praise the Lord in your life, then; 'offer a sacrifice of praise,' (Psalm 49: 14) and thus is shown in your soul the way by which you will come to His salvation."[57]

---

[57] Niceta of Remesiana, *De utilitate hymnorum* 7, in *Music*, p. 136.

B. THE SINGING OF HYMNS

The Singing of Hymns in the Old Testament

The singing of hymns goes back to the earliest days of Scripture. Our first biblical reference is from the Song of Moses, as stated in Exodus 15: 1:

"I will sing to the Lord, for He has triumphed gloriously!"

The same quote is found in his sister's song, the Song of Miriam (Exodus 15: 21). The Israelites, when led to a well, also responded in song:

"Spring up, O well! – Sing to it! – the well that the princes dug, which the nobles of the people delved, with the scepter and with their staves." (Numbers 21: 17-18)

Victorious singing also occurred in the days of the judges. Deborah and Barak rejoiced in their victory over Sisera:

> "Hear, O kings! Give ear, O princes! To the Lord I will sing, I will make melody to the Lord, the God of Israel." (Judges 5: 3)

King David, when he was finally delivered by God from the hands of Saul, also engaged in singing hymns of thanksgiving:

> "For this I will extol You, O Lord, among the nations, and sing praises to Your Name." (2 Samuel 22: 50)

When the ark of the Lord was brought to Jerusalem, musical praise was again given to the Lord:

"Sing to Him, sing praises to Him, tell of all His wonderful works!" (1 Chronicles 16: 9)

"Sing to the Lord, all the Earth! Tell of His salvation from day to day." (1 Chronicles 16: 23)

All of creation joins in this festive song:

"Then will the trees of the wood sing for joy before the Lord, for He comes to judge the Earth!" (1 Chronicles 16: 33)

Song also accompanied the Lord's deliverance of Israel from Moab and Ammon:

> "And when they began to sing and praise, the Lord set an ambush against the men of Ammon, Moab, and Mount Seir, who had come against Judah, so that they were routed." (2 Chronicles 20: 22)

During the reign of the good king, Hezekiah, he gave instruction at the time of the sanctifying of the temple:

> "And Hezekiah the king and the princes commanded the Levites to sing praises to the Lord with the words of David and of Asaph the seer. And they sang praises with gladness, and they bowed down and worshiped." (2 Chronicles 29: 30)

The Psalter and the Singing of Hymns

There are many references to the singing of hymns in the Book of Psalms. The first is found in Psalm 7: 17:

"I will give to the Lord the thanks due to His righteousness, and I will sing praise to the Name of the Lord, the Most High!" Shortly after that, we find: "I will be glad and exult in You, I will sing praise to Your Name, O Most High!" (Psalm 9: 2)

Nine verses later, we read:

"Sing praises to the Lord, Who dwells in Zion! Tell among the peoples His deeds!" (Psalm 9: 11)

Further along, we find: "I will sing to the Lord, because He has dealt bountifully with me." (Psalm 12: 6)

In the rest of the Psalter, there are different Psalms in various categories that refer to the singing of hymns:

- Singing to His Name: Psalms 17: 49; 60: 8; 65: 2, 4; 67: 4; 91: 1; 95: 2; and 134: 3.

- Singing of His mercy: Psalms 58: 16; 88: 1; and 100: 1.

- Singing hymns of joy and rejoicing: Psalms 26: 6; 64: 13; 66: 4; 70: 23; and 97: 4.

- Singing hymns to His power: Psalms 20: 13; and 58:16.

- Singing hymns of praise: Psalms 26: 6; 46: 6 (twice); 46: 7; 56: 7; 56: 9; 74: 9; 107: 1; 107: 3; 137: 1; 143: 9; 145: 2; 147: 1; 147: 7; and 149: 3.

- Singing hymns of His righteousness: Psalm 50: 14; and 144: 17.

- Singing of hymns by His creation: Psalm 103: 12.

- Singing hymns directly of or to God: Psalms 58: 17; 65: 4; 67: 4; 67: 32 (twice); 70: 22; 80: 1; 94: 1; 95: 1 (twice); 97: 1; 97: 5; 100: 1; 103: 33 (twice); 104: 2 (twice); 137: 5; 143: 9; 147: 7; 149: 1; and 149: 5.

The one reference to the singing of hymns in Proverbs is found in 29: 6:

"An evil man is ensnared in his transgressions, but a righteous man sings and rejoices."

The Prophets and the Singing of Hymns

The various prophets of the Old Testament also commented on the singing of hymns.

Isaiah

The greatest of the prophets, Isaiah, first refers to singing in a rebuking analogy of vineyards that yielded wild grapes to being symbols of Judah and Israel:

"Let me sing a song for my beloved, a love song concerning his vineyard (Isaiah 5: 1).

Later, his reference to singing concerns giving glory to God:

"Sing praises to the Lord, for He has done gloriously! Let this be known in all the Earth! Shout, and sing for joy, O inhabitant of Zion, for great in your midst is the Holy One of Israel!" (Isaiah 12: 5-6)

In his prophecy of Tyre being forgotten for seventy years, song is referenced to the end of the seventy years when Tyre will once more be remembered:

"In that day, Tyre will be forgotten for seventy years, like the days of one king. At the end of seventy years, it will happen to Tyre as in the song of the harlot: 'Take a harp, go about the city, O forgotten harlot! Make sweet melody, sing many songs, that you may be remembered.'" (Isaiah 23: 15-16)

In the following chapter, we once again hear about singing in order to give praise and glory to God:

> "They lift up their voices, they sing for joy; over the majesty of the Lord they shout from the west. Therefore, in the east, give glory to the Lord; in the coastlands of the sea, to the Name of the Lord, the God of Israel. From the ends of the Earth we hear songs of praise, of glory to the Righteous One." (Isaiah 24: 14-16)

The singing of hymns is also tied to the future general resurrection:

> "Your dead will live, their bodies will rise. O dwellers in the dust, awake and sing for joy! For, Your dew is a dew of light, and on the land of the shades You will let it fall." (Isaiah 26: 19)

Again, singing is victorious on the day of the Lord:

> "In that day: 'A pleasant vineyard, sing of it! I, the Lord, am its keeper; every moment I water it. Lest any one harm it, I guard it night and day; I have no wrath." (Isaiah 27: 2-3)

Other passages connect singing with the restoration of all things at the future general resurrection:

> "Then the eyes of the blind will be opened, and the ears of the deaf unstopped; then will the lame man leap like a hart, and the tongue of the dumb sing for joy." (Isaiah 35: 5-6)

And, further on:

"Sing to the Lord a new song, His praise from the end of the Earth! Let the sea roar, and all that fills it, the coastlands and their inhabitants. Let the desert and its cities lift up their voice, the villages that Kedar inhabits; let the inhabitants of Sela sing for joy, let them shout from the top of the mountains. Let them give glory to the Lord, and declare His praise in the coastlands. The Lord goes forth like a mighty man, like a man of war He stirs up His fury; He cries out, He shouts aloud, He shows Himself mighty against His foes." (Isaiah 42: 10-13)

Here, the final victory of God over His enemies is clearly apparent.

More passages concerning this victory associate its celebration with singing:

"Sing, O Heavens, for the Lord has done it; shout, O depths of the Earth; break forth into singing, O mountains, O forest, and every tree in it! For, the Lord has redeemed Jacob, and will be glorified in Israel!" (Isaiah 44: 23)

And again:

"Sing for joy, O Heavens, and exult, O Earth; break forth, O mountains, into singing! For, the Lord has comforted His people, and will have compassion on His afflicted." (Isaiah 49: 13)

And again:

"Hark, your watchmen lift up their voice, together they sing for joy; for eye to eye they see the return of the Lord to Zion. Break forth together into singing, you waste places of Jerusalem; for, the Lord has comforted His people, He has redeemed Jerusalem. The Lord has bared His holy arm before the eyes of all the nations; and all the ends of the Earth will see the salvation of our God." (Isaiah 52: 8-10)

And again:

"Sing, O barren one, who did not bear; break forth into singing and cry aloud, you who have not been in travail! For, the children of the desolate one will be more than the children of her who is married, says the Lord." (Isaiah 54: 1)

And finally:

"Therefore, thus says the Lord God: 'Behold, My servants will eat, but you will be hungry; behold, My servants will drink, but you will be thirsty; behold, My servants will rejoice, but you will be put to shame; behold, My servants will sing for gladness of heart, but you will cry out for pain of heart, and will wail for anguish of spirit.'" (Isaiah 65: 13-14)

Jeremiah

Even the prophet Jeremiah, who suffered so much from the disobedience of Israel and Judah that he wrote his Lamentations, acknowledges the joy of the people who sing hymns to God:

"Sing to the Lord; praise the Lord! For, He has delivered the life of the needy from the hand of evildoers." (Jeremiah 20: 13)

Further on, he writes:

"For, thus says the Lord: 'Sing aloud with gladness for Jacob, and raise shout for the chief of the nations; proclaim, give praise, and say, "The Lord has saved His people, the remnant of Israel."'" (Jeremiah 31: 7)

And, just five verses later: "They will come and sing aloud on the height of Zion, and will be radiant over the goodness of the Lord, over the grain, the wine, and the oil, and over the young flock and the herd; their life will be like a watered garden, and they will languish no more." (Jeremiah 31: 12)

Finally, we have this passage:

"Then the Heavens and the Earth, and all that is in them, will sing for joy over Babylon; for, the destroyers will come against them out of the Earth, says the Lord." (Jeremiah 51: 48)

Zephaniah

The prophet Zephaniah has one passage of singing praise to God:

> "Sing aloud, O daughter of Zion; shout, O Israel! Rejoice and exult with all your heart, O daughter of Jerusalem! The Lord has taken away the judgments against you, He has cast out your enemies. The King of Israel, the Lord, is in your midst; you will fear evil no more." (Zephaniah 3: 14-15)

Zechariah

Finally, from the Old Testament, we have the following passage from the prophet, Zechariah:

> "Sing and rejoice, O daughter of Zion; for lo, I come and I will dwell in the midst of you, says the Lord." (Zechariah 3: 10)

The Singing of Hymns in the New Testament

There are just a few passages from the New Testament that touched on the subject of the singing of hymns. The first is from St Paul's Epistle to the Romans:

> "As it is written: 'Therefore, I will praise You among the Gentiles, and sing to Your Name!" (Romans 15: 9)

Then, in a passage referring specifically to liturgical singing in church, St Paul writes:

> "What am I to do? I will pray with the spirit and I will pray with the mind also. I will sing with the spirit and I will sing with the mind also." (1 Corinthians 14: 14-15)

St James, in his Epistle, writes:

> "Is any one among you suffering? Let him pray. Is any cheerful? Let him sing praise." (James 5: 13)

Actually, in this last passage, the RSV is somewhat inaccurate. The Greek original, correctly translated, says, "Is any **joyful**? Let him sing praise."

Finally, from the Book of Revelation, when all is to be fulfilled in the Kingdom of God, we read:

> "And they sing the song of Moses, the servant of God, and the song of the Lamb, saying, 'Great and wonderful are Your deeds, O Lord God the Almighty! Just and true are Your ways, O King of the ages! Who will not fear and glorify Your Name, O Lord? For, You alone are holy. All nations will come and worship You, for Your judgments have been revealed.'" (Revelation 15: 3-4)

The Church Fathers and the Singing of Hymns

The Church fathers commented on the singing of hymns in their writings. Again, we begin with St Basil the Great.

St Basil the Great

Having stressed the importance of the Person of the Holy Spirit in the Holy Trinity in his treatise, ***On the Holy Spirit***, St Basil enumerates the Paraclete's involvement in the creation of music:

> "What did the Holy Spirit do when He saw that the human race was not led easily to virtue, and that, due to our penchant for pleasure, we gave little heed to an upright life? ***He mixed sweetness of melody with doctrine*** so that, inadvertently, we would absorb the benefit of the words through gentleness and ease of hearing, just as clever physicians frequently smear the

cup with honey when giving the fastidious some rather bitter medicine to drink. **Thus, He contrived for us these harmonious Psalm tunes**, so that those who are children in actual age, as well as those who are young in their behavior, while appearing only to sing would in reality be training their souls. For, not one of these many indifferent people ever leaves church easily retaining in memory some maxim of either the Apostles or the prophets, but they do sing the texts of the Psalms at home and circulate them in the marketplace."[58]

St Basil further commends on the connection between singing and doctrine:

---

[58] Basil the Great, *Homilia in psalmum* i, in *Music*, p. 65 (emphasis added).

> "O the wise invention of the teacher who contrives that, ***in our singing, we learn what is profitable, and that, thereby, doctrine is somehow more deeply impressed upon our souls!*** What is learned under duress tends not to be retained, but what suavely ingratiates itself somehow abides within our souls more steadfastly."[59]

He echoes the teaching of St Paul regarding singing with understanding:

> "You have a Psalm, you have a prophecy, you have the Gospel precepts and the pronouncement of the Apostles. ***While your tongue sings, let your mind search out the meaning of the words, so that you might sing in spirit and sing also in***

---

[59] Basil the Great, *Homilia in psalmum* i, 2, in *Music*, p. 66 (emphasis added).

understanding."⁶⁰

He repeats this teaching in one of his published **Canons**:

> "***Those singing Psalms at the altar will not sing with pleasure, but with understanding***; they should sing nothing other than Psalms....The congregation will respond with vigor after every Psalm. If anyone is physically sick, so that he answers after the others, no blame resides in him; but, if he is healthy and keeps quiet, then one leaves him alone; he is not worthy of blessing."⁶¹

---

[60] Basil the Great, *Homilia in psalmum* xxviii, 7, in *Music*, p. 66 (emphasis added).

[61] Basil the Great, *Canon 97*, in *Music*, p. 120 (emphasis added).

Finally, this beloved father associates the singing of hymns on our part with the singing of the angels before God:

> "***What is more blessed than to imitate the chorus of angels here on Earth; to arise for prayer at the very break of day and honor the Creator with hymns and songs***; and then, when the sun shines brightly, to turn to our work and, with prayer as an ever-present companion, to season our tasks with hymns, as if with salt? For, the consolation of hymns favors the soul with a state of happiness and freedom from care."[62]

---

[62] Basil the Great, *Letter II to Gregory of Nazianzus*, 2, in *Music*, p. 68 (emphasis added).

St John Chrysostom

The beloved Church father, St John Chrysostom, also wrote regarding the singing of hymns:

> "Just as He accepted sacrifices while not needing sacrifices – 'If I were hungry,' He says, 'I would not tell you' (Psalm 49: 12) – but rather to lead men to honor Him, **so, too, does He accept hymns while not needing our praise, but rather because He desires our salvation.**"[63]

> "For, we would establish as your teachers in each church the prophets, Apostles, patriarchs, and all righteous men. Yet, nothing more is accomplished by this. Rather, when you are dismissed, **after singing the response to two or three**

---

[63] John Chrysostom, *In psalmum* vii, 15, in *Music*, p. 79 (emphasis added).

> **Psalms** and saying the accustomed prayers superficially and in an indifferent manner, **you consider this to be enough for your salvation.**"[64]

The saint also connects the singing of hymns with the cleansing of the soul:

> "Since this sort of pleasure is natural to our soul, and lest the demons introduce licentious songs and upset everything, God erected the barrier of the Psalms, so that they would be a matter of both pleasure and profit. For, from strange songs, harm and destruction enter in along with many a dread thing, since what is wanton and contrary to the Law in these songs settles in the various parts of the soul, rendering it weak and soft. But, from the spiritual Psalms can come considerable pleasure,

---

[64] John Chrysostom, *In Matthaeum*, Homily XXXi, 2, in *Music*, p. 84 (emphasis added).

much that is useful, much that is holy, and the foundation of all philosophy, ***as these texts cleanse the soul and the Holy Spirit flies swiftly to the soul who sings such songs***."[65]

The holy father even associates the singing of hymns with a call to Christ:

"And let us stand together and say, 'You have made us glad, Lord, in Your work, and in the works of Your hands we will rejoice.' (Psalm 91: 5) And after the psalmody prayer is to be offered, so that we might also sanctify the house itself along with the soul. Just as those who introduce actors, dancers, and prostitutes into banquets, also summon there demons and the devil, and fill their homes with every manner of discord – instances of

---

[65] John Chrysostom, *In psalmum* xli, 1, in *Music*, p. 80 (emphasis added).

jealousy, adultery, fornication, and numerous other dread things – **so those who call upon David with his cithara, call upon Christ inwardly through him.** Where Christ is, no demon would dare enter, indeed none would even dare peep in there; rather would peace, love, and all good things flow as from fountains. Those others make a theatre of their house; you must make a church of your home. For, where there is a Psalm, prayer, the dance of prophets, and a pious attitude among the singers, one would not err in calling such a gathering a church."[66]

St John says that the singing of hymns is a form of praise to God:

---

[66] John Chrysostom, *In psalmum* xli, 2, in *Music*, p. 81 (emphasis added).

"They went out at that time [Palm Sunday] holding palm branches, and they cried out and said: 'Hosanna in the highest! Blest is he who comes in the Name of the Lord!' (Matthew 21: 9) Let us also go out, and, displaying in place of palm branches blossoming good intentions, **let us cry out as we sang today in response: 'Praise the Lord, O my soul! I will praise the Lord as long as I live!'** (Psalm 145: 2) ….But, let us see what he says. 'Praise the Lord, O my soul!' **Let us sing these words today along with David.**"[67]

Finally, St John articulates the connection of the singing of hymns with *nepsis*, that is, watchfulness:

---

[67] St John Chrysostom, *Homilia habita in magnum hebdomadam* 2, in *Music*, p. 83 (emphasis added).

"And these song themselves are appropriate and full of love for God. 'In the night,' he says', lift up your hands to God.' (Psalm 133: 2) And again, 'My spirit rises up early to You from the night, O God, so that the light of Your commandments will be upon the Earth." (Isaiah 26: 9) And the songs of David cause great fountains of tears, whenever he sings these words, 'I am weary with my moaning; every night I flood my bed with tears, I drench my couch with weeping.' (Psalm 6: 7) And again, 'Because I have eaten ashes like bread.' (Psalm 101: 10)... Again when they sing with the angels (for, the angels also sing at that time), saying, 'Praise the Lord from the Heavens' (Psalm 148: 1); as we are yawning, scratching, snoring, or else just flat on our backs, planning myriad empty schemes. **What a thing it is for them to spend the entire night in this**

manner."[68]

C. THE ESSENCE OF SINGING

From everything that has been discussed in this chapter so far, we can draw some very definite conclusions regarding the essence of singing.

Singing as the Highest Form of Verbal Expression

First, we can see that, in the various types of verbal expression, singing is the highest form of such expression. St Clement of Alexandria speaks about the human body being the "instrument" of God:

---

[68] John Chrysostom, *In I Timotheum, Homily XIV*, 4, in *Music*, pp. 87-88 (emphasis added).

"The Spirit, distinguishing the Divine Liturgy from this sort of revelry, sings: 'Praise Him with the sound of the trumpet,' and, indeed, He will raise the dead with the sound of the trumpet. 'Praise Him on the psaltry,' **for the tongue is the psaltry of the Lord**. 'And praise Him on the cithara,' **let the cithara be taken to mean the mouth, played by the Spirit as if by a plectrum**. 'Praise Him with tympanum and chorus' **refers to the Church meditating on the resurrection of the flesh in the resounding membrane**. 'Praise Him on strings and the instrument' **refers to our body as an instrument and its sinews as strings from which derives its harmonious tension, and when strummed by the Spirit it gives off human notes**. 'Praise Him on the clangorous cymbals' **speaks of the tongue as the cymbal of the mouth that sounds as the lips are moved**. Therefore, He called out to all mankind, 'Let every breath praise the Lord,' because He watches over every breathing thing He has made."⁶⁹

St John Chrysostom has similar words to say concerning this:

"Here there is no need of the cithara, nor taut strings, nor the plectrum and technique, nor any sort of instrument; but, if you wish, **make of yourself a cithara, by mortifying the limbs of the flesh and creating full harmony between body and soul. For, when the flesh** does not lust against the Spirit, but **yields to His commands, and perseveres along the path that is noble and admirable, you thus produce a spiritual melody.**"⁷⁰

---

⁶⁹ Clement of Alexandria, *Pedagogus* II, iv, in *Music*, pp. 32-33 (emphasis added).

⁷⁰ John Chrysostom, *In psalmum xli*, 2, in *Music*, p. 81 (emphasis added).

St Athanasius the Great connected music with the spirituality of the soul:

> "Just as we make known and signify the thoughts of the soul through the words we express, so, too, **the Lord wished the melody of the words to be a sign of the spiritual harmony of the soul**, and ordained that the canticles be sung with melody and the Psalms read with song."[71]

The saints also spoke of the unity of the voice and the unity of the spirit. First, St Ignatius of Antioch:

> "Wherefore, it is fitting that you concur with the intention of your bishop, as in

---

[71] Athanasius the Great, *Epistula ad Marcellinum* 28, in *Music*, p. 53 (emphasis added).

fact you do. For, your most renowned presbytery, worthy of God, is attuned to the bishop as strings to a cithara. **Hence, it is that Jesus Christ is sung in your unity of mind and concordant love**. And, to a man, you make up a chorus, so that, **joined together in harmony and having received the godly strain in unison, you might sing in one voice through Jesus Christ to the Father**, that He might hear you and recognize you through your good deeds as members of His Son. It is beneficial, then, for you to be in blameless unity so that you might always partake of God."[72]

Next, we hear from St Justin the Martyr:

"For, neither by nature nor by human understanding is it possible for men to know things so great and divine, but, by

---

[72] Ignatius of Antioch, *Ephesians* IV, 1-2, in *Music*, p. 19 (emphasis added).

the gift descending from above at that time upon these holy men, to whom there was no need of verbal artifice nor of saying anything in a contentious, quarrelsome way, but to present themselves pure to the working of the divine Spirit, so that the Divinity itself, coming down from Heaven like a plectrum and using those just men as an instrument like the cithara or lyre, might reveal to us the knowledge of divine and heavenly things. **Therefore, as from one mouth and one tongue, in conformity and harmony with one another**, they have taught us above God, about the creation of the world, about the fashioning of man...."[73]

---

[73] Justin the Martyr, *Hortatory Address to the Greeks* 8, in *Music*, p. 21 (emphasis added) [attributed to Pseudo-Justin].

Singing with the Angels

When we engage in singing Psalms and hymns, we are united with the singing of the angels in the angelic chorus:

> "***Let us consider the entire multitude of angels, how standing by you they minister to His will***. For, the Scripture says: 'Ten thousand times ten thousand stood by Him and a thousand times a thousand ministered to Him and cried out, "Holy! Holy! Holy is the Lord of Sabaoth! The whole of creation is full of His glory!" (Isaiah 6: 3)' ***Let us, therefore, gathered together in concord by conscience, cry out earnestly to Him as if with one voice, so that we might come to share in His great and glorious promises***."[74]

---

[74] Clement of Rome, *I Corinthians* xxxiv, 5-7, in *Music*, p. 18 (emphasis added).

St Cyril of Jerusalem has no less than three passages connecting our singing with the angelic choir:

> "***Even now, let there ring in your ears that sweet sound that you desire to hear the angels sing after you have been saved***: 'Blest are they whose iniquities are taken away and whose sins are covered,' (Psalm 31: 1) when you enter in, as if stars of the Church, shining in body and luminous in soul."[75]

> "They divide the cloak and cast lots for the tunic. Is this not also written? ***The zealous singers of the Church know, who imitate the angelic hosts and hymn God at all times***; they are found worthy to sing on this Golgotha and say: 'They parted my garments among them, and, for my clothing, they cast lots.' (Psalm 21: 9, quoted in John 19: 24)"[76]

---

[75] Cyril of Jerusalem, *Procatechesis* xv, in *Music*, p. 76 (emphasis added).

"We call to mind the Seraphim also, whom Isaiah saw in the Holy Spirit, present in a circle about the throne of God, covering their faces with two wings, their feet with two, and flying with two, and saying: 'Holy! Holy! Holy is the Lord of hosts!' (Isaiah 6: 3) **Therefore, we recite this doxology transmitted to us by the Seraphim, in order to become participants in the hymnody of the super terrestrial hosts.**"[77]

St John Chrysostom also has a couple of passages regarding the singing of men and the singing of angels:

---

[76] Cyril of Jerusalem, *Catechesis* XIII, 26, in *Music*, p. 76 (emphasis added).

[77] Cyril of Jerusalem, *Mystagogical Catechesis* V, 6, in *Music*, p. 76 (emphasis added).

> "These who are the light of the world, when the sun is up, or rather long before its appearance, rise from bed, healthy, alert, and sober…arising, then, straightway from their beds, radiant and cheerful, they form one choir, and all together in unison and with clear conscience, they sing, as from one mouth, hymns to the God of all, honoring Him and giving Him thanks for every benefit, whether individual or common. ***So, if it seems proper… we will ask what is the difference between a choir of angels and this choir of men on Earth singing the words, 'Glory to God in the highest, and on Earth peace, good will among men!' (Luke 2: 14)***"[78]

> ***"Above, the hosts of angels sing praise; below, men form choirs in the churches and imitate them by singing the same***

---

[78] John Chrysostom, *In Matthaeum*, Homily LXVII, 3, in *Music*, p. 85 (emphasis added).

doxology. Above, the Seraphim cry out in the Tersanctus; below, the human throng sends up the same cry. ***The inhabitants of Heaven and Earth are brought together in a common solemn assembly; there is one thanksgiving, one shout of delight, one joyful chorus.***"[79]

Singing and Joy

It is also obvious from the Tradition that singing is ***very*** closely related to joy, joyfulness, and rejoicing. The Psalms themselves make this connection very directly (in some of these examples, "shouting" and "singing" and "noise" are synonymous, and "joy" and "praise" are synonymous):

---

[79] John Chrysostom, *Homilia I in Oziam seu de Seraphinis* 1, in *Music*, p. 89 (emphasis added).

"But, let all who take refuge in You *rejoice*, let them ever *sing* for *joy*!" (Psalm 5: 11)

"I will be *glad* and exult in You! I will *sing praise* to Your Name, O Most High!" (Psalm 9: 2)

"But, I have trusted in Your steadfast love! My heart will *rejoice* in Your salvation! I will *sing* to the Lord, because He has dealt bountifully with me!" (Psalm 12: 5-6)

"May we *shout* for *joy* over your victory, and, in the Name of our God, set up banners!" (Psalm 19: 5)

"Be glad in the Lord and *rejoice*, O righteous, and *shout* for *joy*, all you upright in heart!" (Psalm 31: 11)

"*Rejoice* in the Lord, O you righteous! *Praise* befits the just! *Praise* the Lord with the lyre, *make melody* to Him with the harp of ten strings! *Sing* to Him a new *song*, play skillfully on the strings, with loud *shouts*!" (Psalm 32: 1-3)

"My soul is feasted as with marrow and fat, and *my mouth praises* You with *joyful* lips!" (Psalm 62: 5)

"For, You have been my Help, and, in the shadow of Your wings, I *sing* for *joy*!" (Psalm 62: 7)

"You make the outgoings of the morning and the evening to *shout* for *joy*!" (Psalm 64: 8)

"They *shout* and *sing* together for *joy*!" (Psalm 64: 13)

"Make a *joyful noise* to God, all the Earth! *Sing* of His Name, give glory to His *praise*!" (Psalm 65: 1)

"Let the nations be glad and *sing* for *joy*!" (Psalm 66: 4)

"But, let the righteous be *joyful*! Let them *exult* before God! Let them be jubilant with *joy*!" (Psalm 67: 3)

"My lips will **shout** for **joy**, when I **sing** praises to You!" (Psalm 70: 23)

"**Sing aloud** to God, our Strength! **Shout** for **joy** to the God of Jacob!" (Psalm 80: 1)

"O come, let us **sing** to the Lord! Let us make a **joyful noise** to the Rock of our salvation!" (Psalm 94: 1) "Let us come into His presence with thanksgiving! Let us make a **joyful noise** to Him with **songs** of **praise**!" (Psalm 94: 2)

"Then will all the trees of the wood **sing** for **joy** before the Lord, for He comes, for He comes to judge the Earth!" (Psalm 95: 12-13)

"Make a *joyful noise* to the Lord, all the Earth! Break forth into *joyous song* and *sing praises*!" (Psalm 97: 4)

"Make a *joyful noise* before the King, the Lord!" (Psalm 97: 6)

"Let the floods clap their hands! Let the hills *sing* for *joy* together before the Lord, for He comes to judge the Earth!" (Psalm 97: 8)

"Make a *joyful noise* to the Lord, all the Earth! Serve the Lord with *gladness*! Come into His presence with *singing*!" (Psalm 99: 1-2)

"So, He led forth His people with *joy*,
His chosen ones with *singing*!"
(Psalm 104: 43)

"And let them offer sacrifices of
thanksgiving, and tell of His deeds
in *songs* of *joy*!" (Psalm 106: 22)

"Let Your priests be clothed with
righteousness, and let Your saints
shout for *joy*!" (Psalm 131: 9)

"Her priests I with clothe with salvation,
and her saints will *shout* for *joy*!"
(Psalm 131: 16)

"***Praise*** the Lord! ***Sing*** to the Lord a new ***song***, His ***praise*** in the assembly of the faithful!" (Psalm 149: 1)

"Let the faithful exult in glory! Let them ***sing*** for ***joy*** on their couches!" (Psalm 149: 5)

The Church fathers also recognized this connection of singing and joy. First, there is St Cyprian of Carthage:

"And since this is a restful holiday and a time of leisure, now as the sun is sinking towards evening, let us spend what remains of the day in ***gladness*** and not allow the hour of repast to go untouched by heavenly grace. Let a ***Psalm be heard*** at the sober banquet, and since your memory is sure and ***your voice pleasant***, undertake this task as is your custom. You will better nurture your friends, if you provide a ***spiritual recital*** for us and beguile our ears with ***sweet religious strains.***"[80]

Then, we have St John Chrysostom:

"***Why do we have hymns?*** Do we not glorify God and give Him thanks that He has at last crowned the departed, that He has freed him from his burdens, and, with fear cast aside, taken him to Himself? ***Is not this why there are hymns? Is not this why there is psalmody? All these are the acts of those who rejoice.*** 'For, is anyone cheerful?' it says, 'Then, let him sing Psalms.' (James 5 13)....Know what it is that you sing on that occasion.

---

[80] Cyprian of Carthage, *Ad Donatum*, xvi, in *Music*, p. 49 (emphasis added).

'Return, O my soul, to your rest. For, the Lord has dealt bountifully with you.' (Psalm 115: 17) And again, 'I will fear no evil, for You are with me.' (Psalm 22: 4) And again, 'You are my Refuge from the trouble that has encompassed me.' (Psalm 31: 7) You should consider what these Psalms mean, but you pay no attention. Instead, you are intoxicated with your grief."[81]

"Hence, in the beginning, there was wailing and lamentation over the dead, but now there are Psalms and hymnody. The Jews, in any case, mourned Jacob for forty days and Moses for a similar number. They grieved because death at that time was death indeed. Now, however, it is not so. Rather, there is hymnody, prayer, and Psalms, as all reveal that there is an element of pleasure in the matter. For,

---

[81] John Chrysostom, *In Hebraeos*, Homily iv.5, in *Music*, p. 88 (emphasis added).

> Psalms are a sign of good cheer, as it is written, 'Is anyone among you cheerful? Let him sing Psalms.' (James 5: 13)"[82]

Thus, we can see by both the witness of Scripture and that of the Church fathers, that singing as an expression of joy, festivity, and celebration, is part and parcel of the Holy Tradition.

---

[82] John Chrysostom, *De sanctis Bernice et Prosdoce* 3, in *Music*, p. 89 (emphasis added).

5

THE LITURGICAL DIMENSION OF ORTHODOX LITURGICAL MUSIC

A. SINGING AND JOY

We begin this chapter with where we ended the last one, with the discussion of singing and joy. Here, the basis for our presentation is the quote from the Letter of James in the New Testament:

> "Is any one among you suffering?
> Let him pray! *Is any one cheerful?*
> *Let him sing praise!*" (James 5: 13)

Again, the word "cheerful" here can more accurately be translated as "joyful." This small verse from the New Testament provides the basis for the specifics and rubrics of our Orthodox liturgical ordo. The entire set of instructions concerning singing, not singing, and so forth are built on this foundational equating of liturgical singing and the liturgical expression of joy, feast, victory, glory, praise, thanksgiving, and celebration.

First of all, as we have said elsewhere,[83] the center of our Orthodox Faith, the nexus of the entire liturgical year and tradition, is the feast of Pascha, the Resurrection of Christ. Pascha is "the Feast of feasts," the central celebration of the primary event of Christianity, Jesus Christ's Resurrection from the dead. This presages our own general resurrection at the Parousia, the Second Coming of Christ. As Fr Alexander Schmemann, rightly called "the father of liturgical theology," has said:

> "This is the starting point of our understanding of the sanctification of time. It is the Orthodox experience, which goes back to the (A)postles themselves, that in the center of our liturgical life, in the very center of that time which we measure as *year*, we find the **Feast of Christ's Resurrection**. What is

---

[83] Cf. Barrett, David, *Liturgical Theology of Orthodox Liturgical Music*, Orthodox Liturgical Press (OLP), Southbury, CT, January 2017, pp. 19-26.

Resurrection? Resurrection is the appearance in this world, completely dominated by time and(,) therefore(,) by death, of life that shall have no end. The One (W)ho (R)ose again from the dead does not die anymore. In this world of ours, not somewhere else, not in any 'other' world, there appeared one morning (S)omeone (W)ho is beyond death and yet *in* our time. This meaning of Christ's Resurrection, this great joy, is the central theme of Christianity; and it has been preserved in its fullness in the liturgy of the Orthodox Church. There is much truth expressed by those who say that the central theme of Orthodoxy, the center of all its experience, the frame of reference for everything else in her, is the **Resurrection of Christ**....Though it may seem strange to you, it is important to realize that every Sunday is a little Easter. I say 'Little Easter,' but it is really 'Great Easter.' Every week the Church comes to the same central experience: 'Having beheld the Resurrection of Christ...' Every Saturday night, when the priest carries the Gospel from the altar to the center of the church, after he has read the Gospel of the Resurrection, the same fundamental fact of our Christian (F)aith is proclaimed: CHRIST IS RISEN!...This is the heart of our (F)aith; and it is only the reference to Pascha, as the end of all merely natural time and the beginning of the *new* time, that we can understand the whole liturgical year."[84]

"The Church is the entrance into the (R)isen life of Christ; it is communion in life eternal, 'joy and peace in the Holy Spirit.' And it is the expectation of the 'day without evening' of the Kingdom; not of any 'other world,' but of the fulfillment of all things and all life in Christ....But(,) I know that in Christ this great Passage, the *Pascha* of the world has begun, that the light of the 'world to come' comes to us in the joy and peace of the Holy Spirit, for *Christ is (R)isen and life reigneth*."[85]

---

[84] Schmemann, Alexander, *Liturgy and Life: Christian Development through Liturgical Experience*, Department of Religious Education, Orthodox Church in America, New York, NY, 1983 (hereafter referred to as "*Liturgy and Life*"), pp. 76-77 (emphasis in the original).

[85] Schmemann, Alexander, *For the Life of the World: Sacraments and Orthodoxy*, SVS Press, Crestwood, NY, 2002

"It is the worship of the Church that was(,) from the very beginning and still is(,) our entrance our entrance into, our communion with, the ***new life of the Kingdom***. It is through her liturgical life that the Church reveals to us something that which 'the ear has not heard, the eye has not seen, and what has not yet entered the heart of man, but which God has prepared for those who love Him.' And(,) in the center of that liturgical life, as its heart and climax, as the sun whose rays penetrate everywhere, stands **Pascha**. It is the door opened every year into the splendor of God's Kingdom, the foretaste of the eternal joy that awaits us, the glory of the victory which already, although invisibly, fills the whole creation: 'death is no more!' The entire worship of the Church is organized around Easter, and(,) therefore(,) the liturgical year, i.e., the sequence of seasons and feasts, becomes a journey, a pilgrimage towards Pascha, the ***End***, which is at the same time the ***Beginning:*** the end of all that which is 'old'; the beginning of the new life, a constant

---

(hereafter referred to as "*For the Life of the World*"), p. 106 (emphasis in the original).

'passage' from 'this world' into the Kingdom already revealed in Christ."[86]

Being the central event in the history of Christianity, Pascha, as "the Feast of feasts," is, therefore, the most *joyous*, the most *festive*, and the most *victorious* feast of the Church year! And, therefore, it is *not* surprising that, for not only Pascha but also the entire period of Bright Week, <u>**all liturgical elements are to be sung**</u>*!!!* There is to be <u>**no**</u> substitution of reading for singing during this liturgical time <u>**at all**</u>*!!* For example, during the course of the regular liturgical year, when parishes have a reader celebrate the 3rd and the 6th Hours before the Sunday Liturgy, all of the Psalms, prayers, troparia, kontakia, and exclamations are read. However, for the **<u>Paschal Hours</u>**, <u>**all**</u> of these elements, except for the priest's exclamations *are <u>sung</u>!!* Furthermore, even after Bright Week, during the remainder of the Paschal season, there is proportionately *more <u>singing</u>* during this time than

---

[86] Schmemann, Alexander, *Great Lent: Journey to Pascha*, SVS Press, Crestwood, NY, 1974 (hereafter referred to as "*Great Lent*"), p. 13 (emphasis in the original).

there is during the remainder of the liturgical year! In contrast to this, during Great Lent, a season of repentance, fasting, and self-examination, when we liturgically experience our exile from God and His Kingdom,[87] there is **less singing** than found during the rest of the liturgical year. Thus, there is a **direct liturgical connection** of singing with **joy!!!**

B.   SINGING AND THANKSGIVING

There is also an obvious connection between **singing** and **thanksgiving**. The central liturgical service of the Orthodox Church is the Divine Liturgy, where we fulfill our membership in the Body of Christ by partaking of Holy Communion, the Eucharist! The word **"eucharist"** means **"thanksgiving."** At the nexus of this service, the Anaphora, this centrality of thanksgiving is most apparent:

---

[87] Schmemann, *Great Lent*, pp. 38-39 and 69.

"It is meet and right to **_hymn_** You, to bless You, to praise You, to **_give thanks_** to You, and to worship You in every place of Your dominion!"[88]

"For all these things we **_give thanks_** to You, and to Your only-begotten Son, and to Your Holy Spirit; for all things of which we know and of which we know not, whether manifest or unseen; and **_we thank You_** for this Liturgy that You have deigned to accept at our hands, though there stand by You thousands of Archangels and hosts of Angels, the Cherubim and the Seraphim, six-winged, many-eyed, who soar aloft, borne on their pinions, **_singing the triumphant hymn, shouting, proclaiming, and saying!_**"[89]

---

[88] *The Divine Liturgy according to St John Chrysostom with appendices*, Orthodox Church in America, St Tikhon's Seminary Press, South Canaan, PA, Second Edition, 1977 (hereafter referred to as "*Divine Liturgy*"), p. 62 (emphasis added).

This connection of singing and thanksgiving has also not been lost on the attention of the Church fathers, as these two texts from St Justin the Martyr attest to:

> "We have been instructed that only the following **worship** [which, naturally, includes **singing**] is worthy of Him, not the consumption by fire of those things created by Him for our nourishment, but the use of them by ourselves and by those in need, while in **gratitude** [that is, **thanksgiving**] to Him we offer solemn prayers and hymns for His creation and for all things leading to good health."[90]

> "And on the day named for the sun [that is, Sunday], there is an **assembly**

---

[89] *Divine Liturgy*, p. 63 (emphasis added).

[90] Justin the Martyr, *Apology* I, 13, in *Music*, p. 20 (emphasis added).

[***the Divine Liturgy***] in one place for all who live in the towns and in the country; and the memoirs of the Apostles and the writings of the prophets are read as long as time permits. Then, when the reader has finished, he who presides speaks, giving admonishment and exhortation to imitate these noble deeds. Then, we all stand together and offer prayers. And when, as we said above, we are finished with the prayers, Bread is brought, and Wine and Water, and he who presides likewise offers prayers and ***thanksgiving***, according to his ability, and the people give their assent by exclaiming, 'Amen!' And there takes place the distribution to each and the partaking of that over which ***thanksgiving*** has been said, and it is brought to those not present by the deacon."[91]

---

[91] Justin the Martyr, *Apology* I, 67, in *Music*, p. 20 (emphasis added).

Again, here, the connection between singing and thanksgiving is made, since the majority of the Divine Liturgy obviously consists in singing.

C. SINGING AND GOD

Various patristic writers also associated *singing* with **God Himself**. Once again, we begin with St Justin the Martyr:

> "Since my spirit was still bursting to hear what was proper to and special about philosophy, I approached a particularly eminent Pythagorean, a man who prided himself greatly on his wisdom. Then, as I conversed with him, indicating that I wished to attend his lectures and to be his disciple, he said, 'What? Are you not acquainted with **music**, astronomy, and geometry? Or do you expect to comprehend what leads to happiness without first hearing what will draw the soul away from sense

objects and render it fit for things of the mind, ***so that it perceives the Beautiful Itself and what is Good Itself?***"[92]

St Clement of Alexandria goes even further, equating Christ as actually being the Music and the Song of God:

> "He Who is from David, yet before him, the Word of God, scorning the lyre and cithara as lifeless instruments, and having rendered harmonious by the Holy Spirit both this cosmos and even man the microcosm, made up of body and soul – He sings to God on His many-voiced instrument and He sings to man, himself an instrument: 'You are My cithara, My aulos, and My temple,' a cithara because of harmony, and aulos because of spirit and a temple because of the word, so that the first might strum, the second might breathe, and the third might encompass the Lord. Now, this David Whom

---

[92] Justin the Martyr, *Dialogue with Trypho* 2, in *Music*, p. 21 (emphasis added).

we mentioned above, a king and citharist, urged them to the truth and dissuaded them from idolatry. Indeed, he was so far from hymning demons that they were actually put to flight by his music, when, simply singing, he healed Saul, who was plagued by them. The Lord made man a beautiful breathing instrument after His own image. **Certainly, <u>He</u> <u>is</u> <u>Himself an</u> all <u>harmonious</u> <u>Instrument</u> of God**, well tuned and holy, the transcendental Wisdom, the heavenly Word....**This is the <u>New</u> <u>Song</u>**, the shining Manifestation among us now of the Word, Who was in the beginning and before the beginning."[93]

St. Clement then goes on to say that the Gospel is the trumpet of Christ:

---

[93] Clement of Alexandria, *Protrepticus* I, 5, 3-7, 3, in *Music*, p. 30 (emphasis added).

> "If the clangorous trumpet, when sounded, assembles the soldiers and announces the ensuing battle, will not **Christ, breathing a _melody of peace unto the ends of the Earth_**, assemble His own peaceful troops? He has assembled then, O man, His bloodless army by His Blood and His Word, and assigned the Kingdom of Heaven to them. **The trumpet of Christ is His Gospel**: He has blown it and we have heard."[94]

Since Christ is the **Word** of God, the holy father, St Clement, forbids the use of musical instruments in church:

---

[94] Clement of Alexandria, *Protrepticus*, XI, 116, 2-3, in *Music*, p. 31.

"The Spirit, distinguishing the Divine Liturgy from this sort of revelry, sings: 'Praise Him with the sound of the trumpet,' and, indeed, He will raise the dead with the sound of the trumpet. 'Praise Him on the psaltry,' *for the tongue is the psaltry of the Lord*. 'And praise Him on the cithara,' *let the cithara be taken to mean the mouth, played by the Spirit as if by a plectrum*. 'Praise Him with tympanum and chorus' *refers to the Church meditating on the resurrection of the flesh in the resounding membrane*. 'Praise Him on strings and the instrument' *refers to our body as an instrument and its sinews as strings from which derives its harmonious tension, and when strummed by the Spirit it gives off human notes*. 'Praise Him on the clangorous cymbals' *speaks of the tongue as the cymbal of the mouth that sounds as the lips are moved*. Therefore, He called out to all mankind, 'Let every breath praise the Lord,' because He watches over every breathing thing He has made."[95]

St Theodoret of Cyrus also bans the use of musical instruments from the liturgical services:

> "Question 107: If songs were invented by unbelievers as a ruse, and introduced to those under the Law because of their simplemindedness, while those under Grace have adopted better practices, unlike those customs just mentioned, why have they used these songs in the churches as did the children of the Law?
>
> "Response: It is not singing, as such, which benefits the childish, but singing with lifeless instruments, and with dancing and finger clappers. Wherefore, the use of such instruments and other things appropriate to those who are childish are dispensed with in the churches **and singing alone has been left over**."[96]

---

[95] Clement of Alexandria, *Pedagogus* II, iv, in *Music*, pp. 32-33 (emphasis added).

D. SINGING AND MAN

The Church fathers also spoke about the relationship between singing and man. They especially associate the human body as being the "instrument" of God:

> "Here, there is no need of the cithara, nor taut strings, nor the plectrum and technique, nor any sort of instrument. But, if you wish, **make yourself an cithara**, by mortifying the limbs of the flesh and **creating full harmony between body and soul**. For, when the flesh does not lust against the spirit, but yields to its commands, and perseveres along the path that is noble and admirable, **you thus produce a spiritual melody**."[97]

---

[96] Theodoret of Cyrus, *Quaestiones et responsiones ad orthodoxos* CVII, in *Music*, p. 107 (emphasis added).

[97] John Chrysostom, *In psalmum* xli, 2, in *Music*, p. 81 (emphasis added).

St Clement of Alexandria even refers to man as an "instrument of peace:"

> "**For, man, in truth, is an instrument of peace**, while the others, if one investigates them, he will find to be instruments of aggression, either inflaming the passions, enkindling lust, or stirring up wrath. The Etruscans, certainly, make use of the trumpet in their wars, the Arcadians the syrinx, the Sicilians the pektis, the Cretans the lyre, the Lacedaemonians the aulos, the Thracians the horn, the Egyptians the Tympanum, and the Arabians the cymbal. We, however, make use of but one instrument, the Word of peace alone by Whom we can honor God, and no longer the ancient psaltery, nor the trumpet, the tympanum and the aulos, as was the custom among those expert in war and those scornful of the fear of God who employed string instruments in their festive gatherings, as if to arouse their remissness of spirit through such rhythms. But, let our geniality in drinking be twofold according to the Law: For, if you love the Lord

your God and then your neighbor, **you should be genial first to God in thanksgiving and psalmody and secondly to your neighbor in dignified friendship."**[98]

Lastly. St Hippolytus of Rome tells us how singing is central to the Divine Liturgy:

"And let them arise, therefore, after supper and pray. Let the boys sing Psalms, the virgins also. And afterwards let the deacon, as he takes the mingled chalice of oblation, say a Psalm from those in which 'Alleluia' is written. And afterwards, if the presbyter so orders, again from these Psalms. And after the bishop has offered the chalice, let him say a Psalm from those appropriate to the chalice – always one with

---

[98] Clement of Alexandria, *Paedagogus*, II, iv, in *Music*, p. 33 (emphasis added).

'Alleluia,' which all say. When they recite the Psalms, let all say 'Alleluia,' which means, 'We praise Him Who is God. Glory and praise to Him Who created the entire world through His work alone.' And, when the Psalm is finished, let him bless the chalice and give of its fragments to all the faithful."[99]

E.   "...AND FOR THOSE WHO SING"

Finally, we see the importance of liturgical singing by the final petition in each and every Litany of Supplication found in all the services:

---

[99] Hippolytus of Rome, *Apostolic Tradition* 25, in *Music*, p. 47 (emphasis added).

> "Again, we pray for those who bring offerings and do good works in this holy and venerable house: For those who labor **_and for those who sing_**, and for all the people here present, who await Your great and rich mercy."[100]

The holy authors who composed and compiled our liturgical services saw and knew the importance of liturgical singing. This petition is proof of that, for, of all the various ministries of the Church, **only the ministry of liturgical singing is specifically mentioned, recognized, and stressed by name in this petition!!!** May those of us who have been gifted with this ministry prove worthy of it, to the glory of God!

---

[100] *Divine Liturgy*, p. 18, and other service books that contain the Litany of Supplication.

BIBLIOGRAPHY

Books

The New Oxford Annotated Bible with the Apocrypha, Expanded Edition, Revised Standard Version, Oxford University Press, New York, NY, 1982.

The Divine Liturgy according to St John Chrysostom with appendices, Orthodox Church in America, St Tikhon's Seminary Press, South Canaan, PA, Second Edition, 1977.

Archimandrite Vasileios, ***Hymn of Entry***, SVS (St Vladimir's Seminary) Press, Crestwood, NY, 1984.

Barrett, David, ***Elementary Music Theory for Orthodox Liturgical Singing***, OLP (Orthodox Liturgical Press), Southbury, CT, January 2015.

_____, ***Liturgics for Orthodox Liturgical Singing, Volume 1*** (July 2015) and ***Volume 2*** (January 2016), OLP, Southbury, CT.

_____, ***Liturgical Theology of Orthodox Liturgical Music***, OLP, Southbury, CT, January 2017.

_____, **Composing and Arranging Orthodox Liturgical Music**, OLP, Southbury, CT, July 2017.

Hopko, Thomas, **The Orthodox Faith: Volume 1: Doctrine and Scripture (An Elementary Handbook on the Orthodox Faith**, SVS Press, Yonkers, NY, 2016.

_____, **The Orthodox Faith: Volume 2: Worship (An Elementary Handbook on the Orthodox Faith**, SVS Press, Yonkers, NY, 2016.

_____, **The Spirit of God**, OLP, Southbury, CT, 2018.

Jordan, James, **Evoking Sound: Fundamentals of Choral Conducting**, Second Edition, Foreword by Morten Lauridsen, with chapters by Robert W. Rumbelow and James Whitbourn, GIA Publications, Inc., Chicago, IL, 2009.

Lossky, Vladimir, **The Mystical Theology of the Eastern Church**, SVS Press, Crestwood, NY, 1976.

McKinnon, James, **Music in Early Christian Literature**, Cambridge University Press, New York, NY, 1987.

The Philokalia: The Complete Text, Volume IV, compiled by St Nikodemos of the Holy Mountain and St Makarios of Corinth, translated from the Greek and edited by G.E.H. Palmer, Philip Sherrard, Kallistos Ware, with the assistance of the Holy Transfiguration Monastery (Brookline), Constantine Cavarnos, Dana Miller, Basil Osborne, and Norman Russell, Faber and Faber, London, England, 1995.

Unseen Warfare, the Spiritual Combat and Path to Paradise of Lorenzo Scupoli, edited by Nikodemos of the Holy Mountain and revised by Theophan the Recluse, translated by e. Kadloubovsky and G.E.H. Palmer, introduction by H.A. Hodges, M.A., D.Phil, Professor of Philosophy, SVS Press, Crestwood, NY, 1978.

Ouspensky, Leonid and Lossky, Vladimir, ***The Meaning of Icons***, trans. G.E.H. Palmer and E. Kadloubovsky, SVS Press, Crestwood, NY, 1982.

Schmemann, Alexander, ***For the Life of the World: Sacraments and Orthodoxy***, SVS Press, Crestwood, NY, 2002.

_____, ***Great Lent: Journey to Pascha***, SVS Press, Crestwood, NY, 1974.

_____, ***Liturgy and Life: Christian Development through Liturgical Experience***, Department of Religious Education, Orthodox Church in America, New York, NY, 1983.

_____, ***Introduction to Liturgical Theology***, SVS Press, Crestwood, NY, 1986.

Taft, Robert F., ***Beyond East and West: Problems in Liturgical Understanding***, Second Revised and Enlarged Edition, Pontifical Oriental Institute, Rome, Italy, 2011.

Articles

Bailey, Mark, "Toward a Living Tradition of Liturgical Music in North America", ***St Vladimir's Theological Quarterly***, Volume 47, Number 2, 2003.

Podcasts

Hopko, Thomas, Podcast series ***Worship in Spirit and Truth***, Ancient Faith Radio.

www.ingramcontent.com/pod-product-compliance
Lightning Source LLC
Chambersburg PA
CBHW071004160426
43193CB00012B/1909